REVOLUTIONS IN EASTERN EUROPE AND THE U.S.S.R.:

Promises vs. Practical
Morality

Edited by
Kenneth W. Thompson

Volume VII
In the Miller Center Series on
A World in Change

UNIVERSITY
PRESS OF
AMERICA

Lanham • New York • London

The Miller Center

Copyright © 1995 by
University Press of America®, Inc.
4720 Boston Way
Lanham, Maryland 20706

3 Henrietta Street
London WC2E 8LU England

Copublished by arrangement with
The Miller Center of Public Affairs,
University of Virginia

The views expressed by the author(s) of this publication do not necessarily represent the opinions of the Miller Center. We hold to Jefferson's dictum that: "Truth is the proper and sufficient antagonist to error, and has nothing to fear from the conflict, unless by human interposition, disarmed of her natural weapons, free argument and debate."

Library of Congress Cataloging-in-Publication Data

Revolutions in Eastern Europe and the U.S.S.R. : promises vs. practical
morality / edited by Kenneth W. Thompson.
    p.   cm. --(Miller Center series on a world in change ; v. 7)
        Includes bibliographical references.
    1. Europe, Eastern--Politics and government--1989- 2. Former Soviet
republics--Politics and government. 3. Post-communism--Europe, Eastern. 4.
Post-communism--Former Soviet republics. I. Thompson, Kenneth W. II.
Series.
    DJ51.R475 1995   947.086--dc20   95-22940 CIP

        ISBN: 0-7618-0049-2 (cloth: alk:ppr)
        ISBN: 0-7618-0050-6 (pbk: alk:ppr)

To those who yearn for freedom
elsewhere in the world, look East:

To
Eastern and Central Europe
and the former Soviet Union
where the struggle is joined
and perils and possibilities
compete for the future

Contents

PREFACE vii

INTRODUCTION ix

I: THE SOVIET UNION IN TRANSITION

1. POLICY-MAKING IN A RAPIDLY CHANGING WORLD:
   THE SOVIET UNION AND EASTERN EUROPE 3
   Nicolai Petro

2. GLIMPSES OF THE OLD AND THE NEW
   SOVIET MIND 21
   Lincoln Landis

3. CHANGE AND THE CONTINUING REVOLUTION
   IN THE SOVIET UNION 35
   Walter Sablinsky, Natalie Kononenko, and Sandra Gubin

II: THE BALKAN EXPERIENCE

4. CHANGE IN EASTERN EUROPE 57
   Daniel N. Nelson

5. THE PRESIDENCY VIEWED FROM EASTERN
   EUROPE: INSTITUTIONAL CHANGE 73
   Eugene Tantchev

III. COUNTRY PROBLEMS AND PERSPECTIVES

6. **CONSTITUTIONAL AND POLITICAL DEVELOPMENTS IN HUNGARY** 91
   Peter Paczolay

7. **IDENTITY CRISIS IN THE CZECH REPUBLIC** 107
   Vladimir Reisky

8. **EASTERN EUROPE: FREE COUNTRIES—CAPTIVE PRESS** 129
   Gene Mater

IV. CHANGE AND REVOLUTION

9. **PRINCIPLES OF 1989: REFLECTIONS ON REVOLUTION** 149
   Steven Lukes

10. **CENTRAL AND EASTERN EUROPE: UNFINISHED REVOLUTIONS** 165
    Daniel N. Nelson

Preface

The literature on the Soviet Union and Eastern Europe is abundant in all but two areas. We have countless books and research projects on the origins, causes, and history of the Cold War. The post-Soviet period has produced numerous studies and publications. If there is a break in the literature, it is the absence of major works on the transition period between the Cold War and the post-Cold War period.

The great merit of the essays in the present volume is their concentration on a neglected period in Russian and Soviet history and change in Eastern Europe. Especially noteworthy is the emphasis authors give to the signs of decline apparent in retrospect but not always recognized at the time. What is revealing is the difference of opinion about the extent of the decline, policies proposed for coping with it, and long-term consequences and implications. The unpredictability of history makes forecasting an uncertain art, yet the diplomat and the statesman must somehow meet the challenge. If the scholar is paralyzed or rendered impotent by the unknown, the policymaker must choose and act, despite limited knowledge and understanding. The luxury that the scholar enjoys of postponing decision making is denied the diplomat and statesman.

The present volume is volume VII in the Miller Center series on A World in Change. The earlier volumes include:

I.   The Presidency in a World in Change
     Edited by Kenneth W. Thompson

II. Development, Decay, and Social Conflict: An
     International and Peruvian Perspective
     By Javier Gonzalo Alcalde

III. New Thinking and Developments in International
Politics: Opportunities and Dangers
Edited by Neal Riemer

IV. Poland in a World in Change: Constitutions, Presidents,
and Politics
Edited by Kenneth W. Thompson

V. Soviet and Post-Soviet Russia in a World in Change
Edited by Allen C. Lynch and Kenneth W. Thompson

VI. Europe and Germany: Unity and Diversity
Edited by Kenneth W. Thompson

Our intention is to complete the series with an additional three to five volumes on Bosnia, NATO, Africa, North Korea, and a second volume on Poland.

Introduction

The attempt to identify and describe the broad outlines of change is often more attainable than the measurement and quantification of change. However, much of contemporary social science proceeds on the assumption that quantification should be the primary goal of social inquiry. Well-financed research projects illustrate this trend as does much of the curriculum-building in universities and colleges.

In contrast, this volume is an old-fashioned study in which seasoned and talented historians, lawyers, political scientists, and linguists seek to make sense of the ever-shifting patterns of change in the transition from the Soviet Union and its satellites to Russia and the former Soviet Republics, and to the recently independent countries of Eastern Europe. The authors trace some of the early responses to forces visible in the late 1980s and early 1990s.

Part I in this volume is focused on the Soviet Union in transition. Professor Nicolai Petro of the University of Rhode Island is an independent-minded interpreter of change in the Soviet Union. Although not a member of any of the prevailing schools of thought, his estimates and appraisals of change put forth in early 1990 appear remarkably close to the mark in forecasting what has happened. Petro's knowledge of Russia and Ukraine uniquely qualifies him for the kind of analysis he offers.

Lincoln Landis viewed change from the border of East Germany. While his academic credentials, including a doctoral degree from Georgetown, are impressive, he also served on the front lines separating the Soviet Union and the West. Like other experienced observers, he displays an ability to use his study and research to assist in an analysis based on experience. Like all good observers, he has "the knack of sizing up events," which is based on a feel for the situation as well as professional knowledge.

The third chapter in Part I examines the historical and cultural realities in the Soviet Union in change. Professor Walter Sablinsky is a historian of Russia and a faculty member of the Department of History at the University of Virginia. Born in Russia, raised in China, and acknowledged to be a master teacher, especially of undergraduate students at the University of Virginia, he provides practical insights on change in the Soviet Union in the light of Russian history. Professor Natalie Kononenko introduces cultural factors that economists and political scientists often overlook. She and her family are part of the *diaspora* from Ukraine to the United States, and she gives the reader a glimpse of what it means to move back and forth from one culture to another and back. Sandra Gubin is a respected and exacting teacher of the government and foreign relations of the former Soviet Union. Whereas Professor Sablinsky is somewhat pessimistic about the future of the former Soviet Union, Professor Gubin is more optimistic. It may be instructive to compare their respective appraisals with what actually has happened in the former Soviet Union and Eastern Europe.

Part II provides a Balkan perspective. It throws the spotlight on Eastern Europe and its institutions, including the presidency. In a wide-ranging and broadly based essay, Dr. Daniel Nelson discusses in chapter four the realities and the impetus for change in Eastern Europe. He analyzes what has been called the *silent revolution* in the 1970s and 1980s in Eastern Europe. In the process, Nelson examines the forces of change, including Gorbachev and U.S. policy. Eventually, he comes to the conclusion that the role of internal causes was primary. Individuals and organizations such as Solidarity in Poland were the most important factors in producing change. The political and economic failures of the regimes generated opposition and brought about change. It was a gradual process and is still continuing. Nelson goes on to discuss the prospects of individual countries in Eastern Europe, including Poland and Czechoslovakia in 1990, Hungary, Romania, Bulgaria, Albania, and Yugoslavia. Nelson helps one see both positive and negative changes in Eastern Europe.

In chapter five, Professor Eugene Tantchev, dean of the Law School at the University of Sofia in Bulgaria, presents a micro-study of the attitudes in Eastern Europe toward government and constitutionalism and the U.S. presidency in particular. His essay is a detailed and well-documented analysis of institutional change throughout the region. Professor Tantchev then reviews the history of presidencies in Eastern Europe. His review is rich in examples of the many varieties, including parliamentary presidents and presidential parliaments. It would be difficult to summarize his perspective on an array of Eastern European regimes, but those who wish to pursue the subject can do so by reading the balance of his chapter.

Hungary played an important role in bringing about change in Eastern and Central Europe. It was a point of passage for some of the refugees who fled communism and sought haven in countries such as West Germany. The draftsmen of a new Hungarian Constitution, including Americans such as Professor A. E. Dick Howard, played a crucial role in the process. They joined with Hungarian legal scholars, including Peter Paczolay, as architects of the constitution. Paczolay describes the role of the courts under the new Hungarian Constitution and the new legal system. His contribution and that of Dean Tantchev highlight the role of law in the furtherance of change, especially in Hungary. He also treats the changing pattern of political parties and the role of former Communists in postrevolutionary governments.

Czechoslovakia and today the Czech Republic and Slovakia have played a historic role in the region. Politically and intellectually, Czech leaders have been the authors of political ideas and institutions that spread across Central and Eastern Europe. Czechs see themselves as heir to the univeralistic traditions of the Austro-Hungarian Empire. They have also been an economic force in the region. The Skoda Works and other industrial centers have made the Czech Republic a force to reckon with. Professor Vladimir Reisky asks whether the Czech Republic, having abandoned some of these historic traditions, can continue to play a vital role in the future. Having set aside some of its ancient traditions, will the Czech Republic discover a new identity, or will it remain subordinate to the great powers in the region?

Gene Mater is a leader in international communication. Formerly with CBS, he has turned his attention more recently to freedom of the press in Eastern and Central Europe. In his essay, he traces the efforts of the state in countries in the region to impose controls over the media and indeed to institute a state information system driving out all manifestations of a free press. He proceeds country by country to identify and explain the differing characteristics of the press and mass media. He accounts for the different institutional patterns. He compares countries in which some measure of freedom of the press has been accomplished with those in which the state remains fully in control. He examines the functions of Radio Free Europe and the role others can continue to play in the post-Cold War world, provided they have not lost relevance. He distinguishes the situation in countries such as China and those of Eastern Europe. His essay is a panoramic view of the media in Eastern Europe.

Steven Lukes is a highly regarded political theorist whose writings in social and political theory have stamped him as a world class scholar. He examines the Revolution of 1989 and seeks to explain why some failed—China and Bulgaria—and others succeeded—Hungary, Poland, and Czechoslovakia. His focus is on the moral dimension of political behavior. Negatively, the revolutions in Eastern and Central Europe came about because of the demoralization of the governing elite. Positively, morally motivated actions played a part in the revolutions. He explores the revolutionary transformations and seeks to explain the political morality of Communist societies up to the point of the transformation. Marxism differs with Western thought in viewing four facts of society as not *necessary* to every society but subject to Marxist historical change: scarcity, particularity, pluralism, and limited rationality. Whereas most societies in the West see such facts as something to which all must adapt, Marxism believes they can be overcome. We see conflicts of interest arising in a struggle over distribution of scarce goods; Marxism sees these conditions as belonging to pre-Marxist history. Marxism is not concerned with rights and justice because the Marxist dialect assures that justice will occur automatically at the end of history. Lukes also asks in the name of what political morality did the revolutions of 1989 occur and under what conditions they can be sustained. His chapter is extraordinarily rich in historical and philosophical analysis.

The concluding essay in this volume is a thoughtful appraisal of the relation between democracy, a free market economy, and security by Professor Nelson. In a commentary on a report in a policy paper series chaired by Rozanne L. Ridgway and John P. Hardt, Dr. Nelson discusses "Unfinished Revolutions" in Central and Eastern Europe. He warns of the limits of external influence over countries in this vast region and urges American officials to practice zero-based policy-making and confront realities in the region. He questions the synergy between democracy and free market systems and writes of a "threat-rich and capacity-poor environment" in present-day Central and Eastern Europe. Both military and political security must exist side by side, and in their absence threats may arise to an emergent democracy and a market economy. This thoughtful yet brief paper brings the volume to a close not with messianic prophecies about a conflict-free world but with serious attention to interrelationships and prerequisites essential to progress.

I.

THE SOVIET UNION IN TRANSITION

Policy-making in a Rapidly Changing World: the Soviet Union and Eastern Europe*

NICOLAI PETRO

NARRATOR: Dr. Nicolai Petro was born in Berlin, the son of a Russian father and a German mother. He received his early education in Italy and came to the University of Virginia where he graduated *summa cum laude* in history. He received a master's degree in public administration and a doctorate degree in foreign affairs. He spent a year at the Miller Center overseeing our Summer Intern Program. He was appointed a professor at the Monterey Institute of International Affairs where he spent three years forming a Russian Studies Center, which has had a wide-ranging and impressive list of publications. He then went to Philadelphia and became a Thornton Hooper Fellow in International Affairs at the Foreign Policy Research Center, for many years an integral part of the University of Pennsylvania but now an autonomous institute. He is currently a Council on Foreign Relations Fellow assigned to the State Department and has asked that I remind everyone that he is speaking entirely as a private scholar and not as a representative of the State Department. He will speak today on policy-making in a rapidly changing world. He will speak in English; however, he knows five separate languages,

---

Presented in a Forum at the Miller Center of Public Affairs on 22 January 1990.

and if he lapses into one or the other of them, we will know the reason. It is a great pleasure to have you with us.

MR. PETRO: Thank you, Mr. Thompson. Policy-making in a rapidly changing environment is the problem that people in government are faced with these days. I came to the State Department in a peculiar capacity, and I suppose that I should start by providing some perspective on what it is that I do there.

The Council on Foreign Relations is a private organization that encourages interesting and fruitful exchanges between academics and policymakers. The Council annually gathers about a dozen academics and places them in government service, while at the same time choosing about a dozen people in government service and placing them in academic institutions; the two then cross-fertilize each other. When I applied, I thought I would be going to the usual institution where people in this program go—that is, the Office of Policy Planning, which does longer-term think pieces. However, the Office of Policy Planning had just hired someone in that capacity. Fortunately, within the State Department there was an office looking for someone—the Office of Soviet Union Affairs. This office, which serves as the motor of U.S.-Soviet relations, was looking for someone in a slightly novel capacity—they wanted to have an in-house policy planner. Policy planners seem to be especially popular these days as many agencies within the U.S. government are starting to think about the longer-term implications of what is happening in the Soviet Union and Eastern Europe and how to deal with them.

My boss recently described what I do as writing policy memos for "the seventh floor." I must admit, however, that from where I sit on the fourth floor, the seventh floor looks a lot farther away than simply three floors up. I have a different definition of what it is that I do: When people ask me, I say, "I think heretical thoughts." I try to put these thoughts on paper and then see where they go within the building and where they finally come to rest. Even so, I remain an academic at heart, and so I would like to share some preliminary observations, perhaps some of them "heretical," regarding how academics and policymakers might help each other in these rapidly shifting times.

4

I have noticed commentary in the press to the effect that the United States, and President Bush in particular, is lagging behind events in Eastern Europe and that the administration lacks a vision and is too cautious. Even after the Malta meeting and subsequent high-level contacts, there is a lingering sense that the United States ought to be doing more. I would like to address these media accusations.

I would like to propose two ideas: First, the United States government, especially this administration, is doing a good job, given the task it faces and the limitations of democratic government. Much of the criticism that is addressed to President Bush in this regard is misplaced because it does not appreciate the proper role of government. In addition, this criticism diverts attention away from the real reason for the United States' lack of creative solutions to events in the Soviet Union and Eastern Europe, namely the inability of traditional sources of intellectual inspiration— academia, think tanks, journals, newspaper columnists—to provide a far-sighted vision of the future role of Russia in world affairs. I think the latter point is cause for particular concern.

Let me briefly discuss the United States government's proper role. The plea to "do something" is little more than a plea for vindication by various factions in the American intellectual community that have debated for generations how to conduct the Cold War. There is a strange coincidence between those new isolationists who see Soviet changes as an excuse to cash in on the "peace dividend" (whose monies have already been spent 10 times over) and those activists who see them as an affirmation of American virtue and idealism. Neither of these factions is really correct.

What is actually unfolding in the Soviet Union is a domestic drama, an internal argument that has remained unresolved since the 19th century. America has contributed very little to resolving this argument, in part because of Russia's self-absorption in domestic political events, such as the October Revolution, the Civil War, the tragedies of forced collectivization and industrialization, and Russia's global competition with the West. The second reason, unfortunately, is that U.S. policies over the past generation have not endeared this country to those who fought for democratic change in

5

the Soviet Union and Eastern Europe. In their eyes, the United States has until now consistently supported the status quo in the Soviet Union and Eastern Europe. The sweeping change in this part of the world has left the United States unclear as to what its main objectives are other than, of course, democracy and better living conditions for the people.

My second idea is that Gorbachev has been able to dominate the world stage precisely because the magnitude of his problems make problems in the United States seem so minor. He faces economic collapse, ethnic civil war, and possibly massive labor unrest. The fact that the spotlight in world affairs has shifted away from the United States and toward him is merely a reflection of the fact that what is happening there is high drama. In contrast, the secondary status of the United States in the global media is partly a reflection of its tranquility, prosperity, and just boring success.

The ability of the United States to react creatively to the events in Eastern Europe is constrained by the functions assigned to governments in a pluralistic democracy. As with most bureaucracies, the government runs by compromises that generally bring creative initiatives down to their lowest common denominator. Anyone who has sat in a committee knows what I mean. From my narrow perspective in one particular office, I have observed many new ideas being generated. There isn't anything I have read about in the press or in any journal that someone in the State Department hasn't already considered. It has even gone beyond simply thinking of these ideas and has tried to give some substance to them by assessing the likely consequences and costs and asking what policies need to be coordinated in order to accomplish the prospective project. Of the mass of paperwork that is generated in creating ideas, however, only a very small part reaches the assistant secretary level, and even a smaller part gets to the secretary of state. Finally, the President makes his decision based not necessarily on the abstract merits of the case as they apply specifically to foreign policy, but perhaps based on some domestic priority: for example, this isn't the right time to push this initiative because it wouldn't "sit right" with this group or that group. All of these things tend to limit truly inspirational thought because a consensus has to be reached.

6

I'm not arguing that things could not be done better. Certain initiatives that the United States finally did take at or after Malta could have been agreed upon earlier. The French did seem to reach a consensus earlier, and the Germans were very much out in front in trying to forge a European consensus on how NATO ought to respond to what was happening in the Soviet Union. Certain types of decision making could be streamlined in the United States, but it pays a price for having the input of so many people at so many different levels of government.

Most of my European counterparts are stunned by the fact that in the United States things are discussed with so many different people, and then they wait and see whether some consensus can be reached. Policy toward the Soviet Union is made by far fewer people in West Germany than it is in this country, and not simply because of the size of that country. It is rather because there is not such a strong imperative to try to get everyone on board. I cannot even write a letter without it being commented upon in three different offices, and if there is any disagreement over the letter we then have to debate it, and one of the principals will have to decide which wording is correct. It is not just because I am a novice—I have actually been given a fair degree of responsibility—but this is simply the way things are done in the State Department and in most other departments in the United States government. The fact that on any serious initiative half a dozen agencies will have to be involved with every level of management represented means that all concerns must be voiced and all concerns must at some point be reconciled. This slows down the creative process.

But doesn't a rapidly changing world environment demand greater flexibility and greater creativity from U.S. foreign policy? Perhaps. Again, however, U.S. foreign policy, as conducted by the State Department, has primarily been to safeguard the nation against possible dangers and *not* to innovate or change the world. In the process of protecting fundamental American interests and values, it is inevitable that some worthwhile ideas are neglected. As an institution the government is only marginally concerned with opportunities lost in the pursuit of safety and stability. This obviously is not a formula for creative success because risks have to be taken if one wants creativity.

I would argue, however, that creativity is not the best measure by which to gauge the success of a nation's foreign policy. Any diplomat will say that diplomacy needs continuity and stability; it entails negotiating over and over the same points so that there is a dialogue, and so that the words that each side uses mean the same thing from one meeting to the next. Navigating uncertain waters in such a way as to enhance American interests is challenge enough for U.S. foreign policies. But I also believe very strongly that in addition to avoiding reefs and shoals, the United States also desperately needs a global map, a vision of the world as we would like to see it a generation from now.

However, this issue is really divorced from everyday policy-making. It is an inappropriate question for government because government is not equipped to handle "the vision thing." Most foreign service officers feel they have enough work in handling day-to-day affairs, and anything beyond is far too speculative and intangible. This task of creating a vision of the world as we would like to see it, therefore, devolves to academics, newspaper columnists, and people in think tanks who I believe tend to lag behind events by six months or more and presently show little sign of catching up.

The most important question that the United States should be addressing now is how it will deal with a Russian federation in the next century (I use the word *Russian* purposely to distinguish it from the word *Soviet*). Disruptions in Central Asia and perhaps in Europe may arise as a result of the diminution of the Soviet Union into some smaller Russian confederation,** and it is to these prospects that the United States must direct its attention. How is the United States preparing for it? Presently the United States is ill-prepared to deal with the emergence of political pluralism and diversity in Russia. U.S. political analysis of the Soviet Union today, I believe, mirrors U.S. economic analysis of that same nation in the mid-1980s: No one at that time had considered the possibility of a transition of centrally planned economies to market mechanisms. It was an interesting philosophical exercise for people

---

**The Soviet Union was formally dissolved at the end of 1991.*

8

Nicolai Petro

who didn't have anything better to do, but it wasn't really a possibility. Therefore, there were neither funds available for it, nor interest in pursuing it.

As a result, the possibility that social discontent could inspire massive political revolt against the governments of Eastern Europe was not even considered by the vast majority of the intellectual community. This fact has serious consequences for the United States today. Because it has so completely missed the underlying currents of Eastern European societies for generations, the single greatest opportunity the United States has for advancing freedom in the latter half of the 20th century might be wasted. The primary impetus for change and the responsibility for transition, of course, rests within those countries. It is also true that academics over these should have been the ones primarily concerned with the possibility of radical change, but too often they expect the United States to have answers to their questions. Unfortunately, the United States is now in the awkward position of not having much to say except, "Don't you understand how markets work? Here's our market, why don't you go and create one like it?"

The United States is facing a big problem called *transition*. The countries of Eastern Europe don't know how to get to the U.S. side from where they are, and the United States doesn't know how to bring them over. Both are looking at this vast, uncharted, and unknown territory and wondering what to do. It is already five to ten years too late. If the United States had had enough lead time to think about the problems of transition to a post-Communist system, arguably it would be that much further along today.

As in Eastern Europe, the United States is also missing the currents underlying the changes in Soviet Russia. We have almost no conceptual framework for the changes there, and with a few exceptions (I would note the work of S. Frederick Starr, the president of Oberlin College, James Billington, the Librarian of Congress, and the works of a few emigré academics), there is little in academic training that can be of assistance.

It is not the government that has failed to provide intellectual guidance, but rather the private, intellectual arena that has traditionally nourished the foreign policy community. Almost all of the serious analysis by Western-based Soviet specialists in their

9

books and articles has focused on how remarkable these changes have been. Very little attempt has been made to explain why these upheavals appeared inevitable and completely understandable to so many people in the Soviet Union and Eastern Europe. These people were not working for a hopeless cause; they believed they would succeed. They may have been surprised at how quickly they succeeded and at how quickly they were thrust into power, but they had an ultimate faith that their cause was the trend of the future. They acted accordingly by trying to establish civic institutions in their own countries.

A recent letter in the *Washington Post* illustrates the tenor of the academic debate in this country. In response to an article by another top scholar, Jerry Hough, one of the most respected Soviet specialists, accused the State Department of fostering "governmental anarchy in the United States; the unwillingness to make decisions, complacency, and this situation should concern us," I believe he has chosen the wrong culprit, however. It is not the government, but the private sector that has the necessary freedom to examine long-range options.

In this regard U.S. scholarship on the Soviet Union compares poorly with what one can read today in leading Soviet journals. People in the Soviet Union are grappling anew with the central issues of Russian history, political culture, and religious and philosophical traditions. A major reason why Soviet analysts in the United States have not provided a coherent vision of what factors will motivate Soviet society in the next century is that they are mesmerized by the actions of a small coterie of political leaders at the very top of Soviet society. U.S. analysis of Soviet affairs overwhelmingly concentrates on Gorbachev: What does he want? What does he think? I call this Copernican Sovietology, because it is focused on the sun; that is, Gorbachev. When he rises the day begins, and when he falls the day ends.

The ridiculousness of this focus could not be more evident than in his recent trip to Lithuania and the way in which it was covered in much of the Western press, particularly by television. Gorbachev's quandaries and difficulties with the Baltic states, his possible intentions, and even his remarks to his wife were given greater attention than the difficult situations that the Baltic leaders themselves faced. Their own analysis of the problems and their solutions were all but ignored. These leaders faced the complex situation of simultaneously reaching an accord with Gorbachev, yet distancing themselves from Soviet control. We lost sight of these important issues during all of this, and instead focused upon whether or not Gorbachev would succeed and what it all meant for his political destiny.

I believe that what scholars need instead of a Copernican approach is a Newtonian approach to Soviet scholarship: one which studies the interaction of a variety of different mechanisms that extend beyond the traditional boundaries of how scholars have studied the Soviet Union for so long. We must move away from a narrow view of the discipline of political science and include the culture, religion, and literature of the Soviet Union as essential to the understanding of political developments there.

The distortion inherent in this top-heavy approach to Soviet society is becoming increasingly apparent if one looks at events in Russia proper. The components of the current political debate are inspired by the Russian literature of the 1950s and the 1960s, the so-called "village prose writers." Today is their political heyday, and anyone who has not read this literature cannot understand the aspirations of the Russian people and why they are on the one hand supporting Gorbachev's limited initiatives and on the other hand arguing for more radical changes in areas like decollectivization and decentralization. They are very fearful of anarchy and bloodshed. Mothers go out and stop their soldier sons from going to fight in Azerbaijan saying, "To heck with it; it's a foreign country. Let them be; we don't need it." The chief of the general staff has had to rescind orders to call up the reserves. This gives one an idea as to the extent of popular discontent in that country.

We have largely missed the significance of the Soviet Parliament. (That is how the Congress of People's Deputies is frequently referred to in the Soviet press, with all the connotations that this word implies.) This Parliament has rejected nine key legislative initiatives advanced by the government; it has rejected Politburo members for Cabinet positions in the last year and has elected a non-Communist minister to the Cabinet. It is significant that in the first free elections held in the Soviet Union in March

1989, the citizens voted overwhelmingly against the Communist party leadership. In the Russian Republic alone, Communist party candidates lost in 76 percent of the districts in which they ran. The only reason that so many Communists are in the Parliament today is because of a prior stipulation that one-third of its delegates must either be members of the party or of party-sponsored institutions. This manipulation, however, will be discarded for the next parliamentary elections.

Unfortunately, American analysts also seem unimpressed by the fact that over one million citizens are now active in over 60,000 informal political associations that form a widespread network across Russia proper. For almost a year now these groups have been coordinating their political platforms in preparation for the local elections of March 1990. The common assumption in the West, however, is that Gorbachev's fate determines the fate of perestroika, despite all of the evidence to the contrary one sees when one looks beneath the surface. This view predominates, and it is wrong. I strongly suspect that in the 1990s people will eventually have to acknowledge that in the Soviet Union, as in this country, all politics is local.

Academics and other observers generally have the freedom to pursue their vision. In too many instances, however, a too-narrow training and expertise impedes their ability to envision an expansive long-range future. By contrast, people working in the government thirst for such a vision. The proliferation of policy-planning agencies at every level of government is a reflection of the fact that they don't see anything useful coming from academics. Unfortunately, I have to concur with my boss that the overwhelming majority of academic work sent to our office for review is "gobbledy gook." There is little that I can use, little that moves us to say, "Now that's a good idea," or "That's a good vision of what the government could do to achieve some stability in the international arena 10 or 15 years from now, given the trends that we see in world affairs."

What is needed is a reexamination of long-standing assumptions about Russian and Eastern European cultures. It is revealing, for example, that a leading Sovietologist has remarked—only half facetiously—that while all Sinologists love

China, all Sovietologists hate Russia. This attitude will have to change before we can begin to appreciate the magnitude of what is happening in world history. What people are actually witnessing is the slow but inexorable return of Russia to the European family of nations. The United States will have to understand the full historical, cultural, religious, and philosophical dimensions of this restoration before it can even begin to appreciate what this change will mean for this country, for it does have serious implications.

There is often a facile assumption that American cultural values have leaped over the great divide of the oceans and embedded themselves firmly into foreign soil. That is not the case. I think America's cultural influence on the rest of the world is largely superficial, and there could very quickly be a backlash against it, the kind of backlash that many have seen, unfortunately, in some large countries in the Third World. I am not saying that the peoples of Eastern Europe and the Soviet Union will necessarily become anti-American, but some basic American values are not entirely consonant with the rediscovery of those nations' historical identities. It is incumbent upon the United States to make the extra effort to understand them, as they will be too absorbed in the process of national revival to make much of an effort to understand this country.

QUESTION: One of the compelling reasons for conservatism in U.S. policy is that the Soviet Union is a nuclear power. How much of a concern is it that, given the Soviet Union's unstable nationalities situation, some of the Soviets' nuclear assets could fall into the hands of one or more of the feuding nationalities? With the danger of civil war present, world security would actually be an issue. Is that area discussed?

MR. PETRO: Yes, it is discussed. I have seen the idea in the press. The United States can do very little about it one way or the other. The United States is not going to be able to hold the Soviet empire together, just as the United States really could not effectively encourage its disintegration; it acts on its own impetus. This problem is really not qualitatively different from the problem of terrorism in general.

If there is going to be a relatively stable transition to another authority in the Soviet Union, then no problems should arise. If irresponsible leaders emerge and get hold of such weapons, however, it is the same sort of problem that the United States has envisioned as to what might happen if a nuclear weapon gets in the hands of terrorists. There is not much to speculate about, for there is nothing the United States could really do in that case. It is a contingency we shall deal with. I suppose the central government of the Soviet Union would be very concerned and would take all steps necessary to prevent this from happening.

QUESTION: In Helene Carrere D'encausse's book, *The Decline of an Empire*, which was published a few years ago, she mentioned that the Soviet Union was on the verge of self-destruction because of nationalities problems. All of the academics that I know thought the book was sensationalist. In retrospect, however, she seems to be more in the ballpark than any of the other academics that I know. How was this book received by the State Department?

MR. PETRO: It is hard to speak for thousands of foreign service officers, but I know that people at the State Department tend to be well-informed about day-to-day events in the Soviet Union and have their own opinions about long-term prospects. The thesis of the book, that the Soviet empire is liable to collapse, is not unique to her, but has been suggested before. It hasn't materialized yet.

What is surprising is the rapidity with which events have occurred. In Russia, however, they have a saying about not whistling at people's graves before they are actually buried. Yes, things are happening in the margins (I don't argue that Lithuanians are marginal in any way): at the outer rim of the empire the world is seeing tensions and separatist aspirations. The sources of those tensions in the Baltic states, however, are very different than those in Azerbaijan. The way Armenians view their ties with the Soviet Union is very different from the way that, say, Georgians view their ties with the Soviet Union. Until quite recently, polls indicated that only 2 percent of Armenians wanted to secede from the Soviet Union. By contrast, in Azerbaijan a much larger proportion favor independence, as they do in Georgia and the Baltic states.

14

There is debate all over the world as to whether the separation of certain regions is something the Soviet government will live with, or whether Moscow is going to fight it tooth and nail. Each interpretation has its own consequences. I think things will proceed on a case-by-case basis. Ukraine and Byelorussia will be the largest problem areas, although aspirations for separatism there are also among the weakest right now for a variety of historical, religious, and cultural reasons.

Senior officials in the State Department usually don't get to read more than two pages on any particular subject. Any memo written for the Secretary has to be two pages or less, and you only get to put forth or react to one idea. To the extent that there is time to read books, I would hope they would be books dealing with what U.S. policy might be in a very different world environment from the one that we are now seeing. As a point of speculative departure, I would set the stage with a Russian federation that has essentially abandoned foreign adventures, given up much of its empire, and wants to live in that global context. That is still a radical thought today. Most Western analysts are still working on the old assumption that Gorbachev is the best Russian available and the Russian people want to hold together the empire at all costs. While this assumption may be true of the political leadership, I think such attitudes are less and less prevalent among the Russian population.

QUESTION: Many years ago, "Mr. X" [George F. Kennan] predicted that due to ethnic, linguistic, and cultural differences, the Soviet empire would eventually mellow. His article predicted this mellowing would happen in 10 to 15 years, but in fact it has taken over 40 years. You seem overwhelmed by this, yet hasn't this mellowing of the Soviet empire been a major goal of U.S. containment policy from the beginning?

MR. PETRO: I agree. To a certain extent, what people are seeing is a vindication of containment. The specifics of what Mr. Kennan thought about containment and its implementation, however, are still subject to differing interpretations.

15

Having said that, it is time to move on to the question of what values will replace those that the United States thought dominated the political system of the Russian heartland. That is a difficult and tremendously important question. The United States needs to understand the values and the fundamental aspirations of the people who will be coming to power in the next generation in an entirely different political environment. No one lives forever, so whether it is one year or 20 years from now, eventually Gorbachev will fall.

What the United States needs to know is whether the institutions that he has established form a sufficient basis for a different evolution of the Soviet political system. I know that this area engenders tremendous debate; very erudite people argue many different aspects of this. I am impressed, however, by the psychological changes that have already occurred, regardless of whether the institutions themselves are seen as solidly entrenched. The Soviet Communist Youth League, for example, is the breeding ground for the future leaders of the Communist party of the Soviet Union. In just four years the Communist Youth League has lost 10 million members, four million of which were lost in 1989 alone. At this rate the Communist Youth League will eventually have no members. In Lithuania, the Communist Youth League has already disbanded, and similar moves are underway in the other Baltic states. In the Russian Republic there is a move to replace the Communist Youth League with a Russian Federation of Youth, very much like what they have in Hungary today.

We are talking about the future leaders of the Soviet Union. We should be considering not only what the people in power today will be thinking about for the next five years, but also what the people who are now in their 20s and 30s will do with the inheritance left to them when they occupy positions of power. This inheritance may be abysmal, but the values, ideas, and inspirations that these new leaders will rely upon is important. It is certainly not too early to think about what those might be.

QUESTION: As for your disappointment with the academic community, I think that your expectations were entirely too high. I understand that the literature and culture of a society affects its politics and its economics, yet don't you underestimate the effects of global trends and ideas upon a society's politics and economics? The world is becoming a place where cultures are interchanged.

MR. PETRO: If my expectations are high, I plead guilty; I went to the University of Virginia. With regard to global ideas versus national ideas, there will certainly be a tremendous number of intellectual influences upon the people of Eastern Europe and the Soviet Union. They will be open to ideas from their Western counterparts and others. However, one of the strong motivating forces in the current reform movement is a rediscovery of their own cultural roots. I believe that this rediscovery will be a dominant political force. For the near future, I suspect that this rediscovery will be more important and will find a greater political resonance than will global influences. What sort of political parties are going to emerge? What will motivate them? Which ones will be popular? Who will their leaders going to be?

Political parties are already developing. By the end of the year Estonia and Lithuania will have multiparty parliaments, and Latvia will probably have one as well. All indications are that Estonia will have about 10 or 12 different parties ranging across the entire political spectrum, similar in political philosophy to parties elsewhere in Europe. Nationalism has been a leading force inspiring the popular fronts, but it should not have a negative connotation. It is an attempt to recapture the values that were lost in the pursuit of an internationalist, Soviet model of development.

That is why I have focused my own research interests on that particular aspect. I may be wrong; there is no doubt that these people are seeking inspirations from every possible source, yet they are also seeking inspiration from their own past historical traditions that they are just now rediscovering.

QUESTION: The United States has never recognized the incorporation of the Baltic states into the Soviet Union. It has also denounced the subjugation of the nations of Eastern Europe by the Soviet Union. If I understand you, U.S. government's policies in this area are based on the assumption that the Soviet empire will eventually collapse. If so, won't the United States soon find itself in a policy dilemma? That is, will the United States soon have to consider all 15 republics of the Soviet Union as potentially independent states, similar to those in the Baltic? Or is the United States assuming that Moscow will be able to stitch together some type of federal Russian state? What is the vision of the nationalities problem upon which U.S. policies are based?

MR. PETRO: Let me say that I am speaking as an academic and my ruminations are my own. I don't wish to imply that there is any consensus of opinion in the State Department about whether the Soviet Union is going to hold together or collapse. That having been said, I can address the specific issue of the Baltic states, because as Secretary Armitage pointed out, United States policy officially does not recognize the annexation of the three Baltic republics.

The United States has implicitly viewed those states in a different category than the individual republics of the Soviet Union. In official press statements the United States reacted relatively mildly to the Soviet military intervention in Azerbaijan, but it would be a different story if Gorbachev were to fail in his efforts in the Baltic states and conflict erupted. It is obvious that the United States government is assessing the contingencies that may arise in the interim until it is possible for one or more of those republics to declare independence and establish themselves as sovereign nations again. That area is where most of the government's attention is focused right now: What will happen, when is it likely to happen, the possible Soviet response, and the possible U.S. counter-response.

QUESTION: What do you think the Soviet interests in Cuba and the Third World will be in the future?

MR. PETRO: I think that the Soviets can be expected to withdraw. We are noticing that the Soviets are turning inward, at the expense of their foreign commitments. This is proceeding at different rates in different countries. In addition to obvious gestures such as the withdrawal of troops, a reduction of foreign aid, or the stopping of arm shipments, it is significant that there now seems to be a lack of ideological commitment in their foreign policy. Domestic discussions center on questioning the utility of foreign aid when so many problems exist within the Soviet Union itself. Even aid to specific allies such as Nicaragua and Cuba is questioned. Private academics are the ones doing this questioning, but they hold very prominent and responsible positions, and their views get aired in the press. Obviously, such statements are partly designed to influence thinking in the United States, but mainly to influence the thinking of people in the Soviet Union.

In addition, there seems to be a concerted effort regarding Eastern Europe. Gorbachev is doing more than just sitting back and watching events unfold in Eastern Europe; he seems to have played some role in encouraging this process at key points, allowing the democrats to win by his action or his inaction. Some indication of this role is seen in other countries as well. The tenor of the dialogue that the Soviets have with the governments of client states and local Communist parties now reflects a differing set of expectations between the Soviet Union and those client states. That is very encouraging. It is obvious, however, that if a regime has either a popular backing or a solid grip on the instruments of control, the Soviet Union is not going to liberate that nation from communism. Thus, there is no basis for predicting that Castro will fall within a particular time frame. One might surmise that U.S. lack of foresight in Eastern Europe could be matched by a lack of foresight in other areas.

QUESTION: Is there not a correlation between the level of education in dictatorial countries and what the world is seeing now? Haven't the Russians sown the seeds of revolt by elevating the education of its masses? Does not communism work best when the peasantry is uneducated?

MR. PETRO: I believe that anyone who is exposed to a greater variety of ideas is going to compare them. I'm not sure that the peasants were ever that dumb. After all, they fought collectivization and paid with their lives. Some estimates of the loss of life go as high as 20 million. One is reminded of Stalin's famous response when Churchill remarked how terrible it was that so many Soviet citizens had been lost in the struggle against the Germans. Stalin replied that fighting the peasants in his own country was a *real* war.

It is true that the country's leaders tend to be better educated. I would find it to be a better way of enhancing the prospects for democracy in any nation, however, if those intellectually inspired leaders actually listened to the people on the bottom. They may not be able to articulate their ideas as well, but they know what they want. They want to be able to till their own land and sell their own goods without suffering these problems that are constantly imposed upon them by the bureaucracy. If one wants to see an example of instinctive democracy in action from (so to speak) the lowest intellectual social class in the Soviet Union, look at the two million miners that coordinated their activities last July and basically shut down the country. They soon came out with political demands, the first of which was to abolish Article Six of the Constitution, which stipulates the guiding role of the Communist party. Later, sections of that movement made even more specific political demands, such as the removal of the Politburo. These miners didn't have any intellectual inspiration. As a matter of fact, they rather frowned on intellectuals telling them what to do because they themselves knew what to do.

NARRATOR: When Nick Petro was at the Miller Center, he distinguished himself by wanting to get inside the Carter and Reagan administrations to see how they administered their human rights policy, and he wrote a little book called *The Predicament of Human Rights: The Carter and Reagan Policies.* Now he is inside the State Department, although he is still an academic and perhaps a "renegade egghead." That kind of blending of policy-making and academic perspective is certainly one thing we would hope that the Miller Center could encourage young people to consider for many years to come. Professor Petro, you have more than lived up to our expectations, and we wish you well in what promises to be a career of accomplishment and leadership.

CHAPTER TWO

Glimpses of the Old and the New Soviet Mind*

LINCOLN LANDIS

NARRATOR: Lincoln Landis has had unique opportunities to observe the Soviet Union. With few instructions he operated on the East German border after World War II. In this front line diplomacy Dr. Landis used his background of a doctorate in government from Georgetown, a master's degree in Russian studies from the Russian Institute at Columbia, and a bachelor of science degree from West Point.

He is a retired lieutenant colonel. He has been active in both the public sector and the private sector. His unique experiences will broaden our understanding of this complex world in the East.

MR. LANDIS: I am aware of the interest the Miller Center has in governance. This year in particular, issues in America's own foreign policy are in flux because of the confusion of fast-moving events in the former Soviet Union.

This problem exists, in my view, because the United States has not paid sufficient attention to the Soviet mind. Now this country wants to know the prospects for success of democracy, especially in Russia, Ukraine, and Belarus, the major republics that have emerged out of the Soviet Union. Economists will have to wrestle with the prodigious task of how to move from a command economy to a free market. I would like to propose just as important a task

---

Presented in a Forum at the Miller Center of Public Affairs on 5 February 1992.

for us, which is to understand what the attitudes are of the people and the leaders who will make a democracy work.

Government assignments have placed me in one-on-one relationships with Soviet citizens going back nearly half a century. These one-on-one meetings yield impressions that are useful glimpses of the Soviet mind. With regard to the new Soviet mind, I am referring to Gorbachev's frequent reference to *new thinking*. He has used this term when speaking of various reforms as in his widely publicized appearance before the United Nations several years ago. I plan to deal with the *new thinking* later, but for now I will discuss the Soviet mind as it has been for some years now.

Some good clues to Soviet intentions are revealed in Soviet behavior and history. They suggest a severe tension on the one hand between the people and the regime, and between the leaders and their formal beliefs. Among ordinary citizens and the privileged alike, there is a remarkable pattern: on the surface, a veneer of conformity, sometimes leading to arrogance and hostility; and underneath, spontaneous good humor.

My observations started to take shape when I joined the Army of Occupation in Germany after World War II. At that time, the United States didn't know if the Russians were its friends or enemies. My instructions as new chief of a Russian liaison team on the border between the American and Soviet zones were "just get out there and liaise!" That was our charter. Along with my sergeants, who were interpreters of Ukrainian descent and came from western Pennsylvania, I set out "to liaise." My team was unarmed and had no credentials, though we were told that we had diplomatic immunity. Our documentation consisted only of the front bumper of my jeep, on which was painted *Russko-Amerikanskaya Svyaz*, Russian American liaison, in large bright letters.

I made a routine visit to the border after the 1948 Berlin airlift had begun. The Russians were thought to have reacted negatively to America's going to the air to defeat their blockade, and when I visited the border, I didn't know if they would be hostile or not. One of the airlift corridors went over the place where I met the Russians, and as usual, a surly sentinel was on duty, glowering at me. Suddenly, one of the American cargo planes appeared overhead, and the soldier looked up with a big grin on his face. He pointed and shouted the only English he knew, which was "Amerikanski C-47!" *His hostility suddenly changed to friendliness.*

In another incident, my sergeant and I were taken at gunpoint by a Russian captain and his patrol of seven or eight soldiers, paying no attention to our diplomatic immunity. I objected when his driver started stripping the gears of my jeep, and to my surprise, he agreed with me and let my sergeant drive.

Back in the headquarters, I prevailed upon the Soviet commandant to allow me to call my counterpart, who told him to let us go. At this point my sergeant and I complained that we were hungry and wanted to be fed lunch. After first objecting, the commandant took us into his office and began telling us Russian army jokes. Soon his orderly served us a tasty two-course meal—meat and potato soup, and the same meat and potatoes on a plate. *In a few hours, our treatment changed from hostility to friendliness.*

Several years later, during detente, I was a civilian adviser to the White House, working on Soviet exchanges to America. One prominent official, who was critical of American business practices during the work sessions, came to me at the end of the week and asked if I would take his group to a large shopping mall outside Washington. They had been saving their scarce dollars to spend shopping, which was the zenith of their trip. *They changed from arrogant visitors to friendly guests.*

On another occasion, a prominent Soviet diplomat appeared on an American talk show and was critical of U.S. policies. A caller asked if he had ever considered defecting. The diplomat, who was well known for his mastery of English, hesitated, and instead of saying, "That's absurd," appeared as if he were thinking about it. Then he composed himself and said, "You should not ask indiscreet questions." *His pretense gave way to frankness.*

A colleague of mine visiting the Soviet Union during the Gorbachev era told of a young lady Communist guide who had been praising the Soviet Union during the tour. When they were ready to depart from the Soviet Union, one American tourist asked her, "Why don't you leave us with a typical Russian joke." The guide paused and said, "Here in Russia the joke is on the people." *Candor replaced pretentious behavior.*

These episodes suggest the lack of legitimacy of the Soviet system. The regime denied people their instinct for spontaneity and individual thought, and the regime's contempt for the people was matched by their contempt for the regime.

History confirms the illegitimacy of the Soviet system. It was born in a 1917 *coup d'etat* that called itself a revolution. It produced, in my view, a behavioral disorder in all of the leaders from Lenin to the present, a behavioral disorder blending pretense with deception. The leaders of the Soviet Union, whatever their reputation, were intelligent enough to recognize that the Bolshevik Revolution canceled out Marxism.

Marx said that a revolution would occur in a proletarian society. Russia in 1917, however, was a largely rural country with a small working class. These leaders have also been well aware that Lenin uprooted a fledgling democracy with his October Revolution. The provisional government, having ousted the czar, had already achieved the top Bolshevik priority.

This Leninist pretense was evident in the leaders' reverence toward Marxism, and Leninist deception was clear as they pursued the end, regardless of the means, to support a fraudulent regime. From day one, in my view, they were not out to conquer the world, despite conventional wisdom to that effect.

Instead, they recognized that the real threat to Communist rule lay in individual rights, diversity, and democratic pluralism. With Leninist pretense they continued to give lip service to the idea of world revolution. This deception extended right down the line of Soviet leaders, in "peaceful coexistence" and detente, and in military efforts to subvert and outflank democratic countries.

Meanwhile, Western policies through the years have enabled Soviet leaders to stabilize their politics at home and abroad. This began, in my view, with the massive demobilization of American forces at the end of World War II. This demobilization sent a likely signal to Stalin that the West would not seriously interfere with his growing hold on Eastern Europe. Soviet provocative actions that followed were not met with any kind of direct confrontation by the West. During the 1948 Berlin blockade, for example, the United

States went to the air in a commendable operation and superb technological achievement but avoided challenging the blockade on the ground.

In 1953 when the Russians brutally suppressed the riots in East Berlin after Stalin's death, there was no reaction from the West. In 1956 during the Polish strikes and the Hungarian revolution, there was no challenge by the West. Likewise, the military intervention in Czechoslovakia in 1968 went unopposed. This pattern was not lost on the Soviet leadership.

I would now like to talk about the third generation Leninists: Gorbachev, Yeltsin, Shevardnadze, and others. From childhood, they learned that party loyalty was the only way to a secure and successful career. They also knew that centralized power was the secret to orderly governance.

On the domestic scene, the people had no opportunity to demonstrate any kind of initiative. Only black marketers could exercise business practices. Thus, the pretense of Marxism continued to exist side by side with efforts to tinker with capitalism and subvert the West through diplomacy and arms control. As this situation took place, Western ideas became a growing threat as Gorbachev emerged as a major actor in world politics. The notion that Western ideas would eventually threaten the Soviet Union in a shrinking world of transportation and communication developments has, I believe, been on the minds of Soviet leaders for decades.

As an economic reformer, Gorbachev was no match for his predecessors. Lenin brought in the New Economic Policy—pure capitalism—in the early 1920s. Stalin started anti-Marxian incentive pay based on output while in democratic countries businesses were starting to pay by the hour, more or less a socialist concept. Later, Khrushchev proceeded to decentralize the economy. Until the August coup, Gorbachev continued to talk about decentralization without seriously doing it. Old codger Brezhnev, who was supposedly no reformer at all, introduced corporate structures that were quite significant in increasing productivity in the Soviet Union.

I would like to briefly refer again to the failure of U.S. experts to predict the Communist collapse. An appreciation of the Soviet mind offers some explanations here. The bilateral exchanges the

United States had under detente created intellectual ferment within the Soviet Union, particularly after Chernobyl. I think the leaders' worst fears, with Gorbachev in the saddle, were threatening to be realized: that in a shrinking world, Western ideas were likely to bear bitter fruit with glasnost in the guise of "openness."

Few in the West understand that glasnost means authorized self-criticism or publicity. It does not mean openness. This mistake had an ironic result. The Western definition of glasnost returned to the Soviet Union via Europe with a devastating effect: People in the streets began thinking *otkrovennost*, the real word for openness. The result was the demise of Eastern European Communist regimes, the mass exodus of East Germans through the newly opened Hungarian border to the West, the toppling of the Berlin Wall, the dissolution of the Warsaw Pact, and the collapse of the Soviet Union. Gorbachev could prevent none of these actions and apparently his prudent inaction qualified him for the Nobel Prize.

Gorbachev's new thinking sounded democratic, but it still did not tamper with the concept of central control. As everyone now knows, that led to his downfall. He insisted on a central Soviet Union to the end. But to make it even more clear, when Gorbachev returned to Moscow after the August coup, he appeared on national television, disheveled, and one would suppose, at his most sincere. He said, "Now we are going to proceed with building democracy, and the first step will be to renew the Communist party." This comment is vintage Leninist, and it tells much about Gorbachev.

Unfortunately, the Soviet mind has outlasted the Soviet Union. The mental residue of the Communist system still exists from top to bottom. As Vitaly Korotich, a reform journalist and editor of *Ogonyok* (the *Spark*), a leading Russian publication, has said that Gorbachev and all citizens down to the last child are not only products of the system, but also its victims.

Like Gorbachev, the ex-Communist leaders of the newly independent republics—Russia, Ukraine, Belarus—also have a big stake in central control. If somehow progress is made toward establishing a free market despite this disadvantage, these leaders still have to address the effect of communism on their constituents:

Lack of incentive, mistrust of one another, habitual fear, and low self-esteem form a poor foundation on which to build democracy. Nonetheless, I do believe that the people of Russia, Ukraine, and Belarus are endowed with the potential to prosper in a democratic society, and in the long run they will free themselves from the reins of the Soviet mind.

QUESTION: Can you give us a glimpse into Boris Yeltsin's mind?

MR. LANDIS: Mr. Yeltsin is a career Communist. All he knew until the age of 55 was the Communist party. His reputation is that of a maverick. For that reason, Yeltsin would never have made it to the top slot as Gorbachev did. But because he is a maverick, I think there is cause for optimism about Yeltsin. He certainly has great charisma and, I believe, great sincerity. While he has changed his mind, he and his advisers still know little about democracy. So he has to depend upon Harvard professors and others who are not Russians. Yeltsin has a terrifically difficult job, to say nothing of behind-the-scenes pressures that may exist for a greater military presence and pressure on the leadership by the Soviet armed forces.

Yeltsin is the best thing that could have happened to Russia at this time. It has to be an ex-Communist to provide leadership. No one else has that kind of stature or experience. Yeltsin does appear to have seen the light, but he still knows nothing about democracy.

The problem is that he's 61 years old, and he might not be counted on for that many more years as an active leader. The ideal situation would be a 45-year-old Yeltsin with time and energy to develop the confidence of the Russian people so that they have continuity without the disruptions caused by change.

When they went to the streets in August, they were delighted that here, suddenly, was an entirely new picture. Yeltsin was a national hero. Gorbachev had not been popular for years because he has been this way and that, talking openness in the West but not truly creating it in the East. I'm optimistic, however, that Yeltsin is a real leader and the best that is available.

27

QUESTION: How much and what kind of foreign aid should the United States provide for the new Russian republics?

MR. LANDIS: The United States has been doing it very well, so far; that is, it has limited it pretty much to humanitarian and medical kinds of help. America has to be careful, because first of all, we don't know the situation there very well. Second, it is a matter of what the United States can afford in this particular time frame of its own economic worries. I think the United States has done well so far and should continue to apply pressure in the sense that it expects concrete progress toward democracy.

Fred Ikle came out with an interesting proposal recently that suggested trying to build on relationships the United States already has between the Soviet military command and the American military command. Ikle, who was the adviser on defense matters and international security affairs for Reagan and is now retired, apparently thinks that there should be some meeting of the minds between Soviet high-level military and American high-level military. He argues that one of the reasons this method might succeed is that the United States has never fought the Russians. The Russian people and leaders have a great respect for America, and with the collapse of their system, they look to America for guidance.

QUESTION: It seems that the United States is focusing on Russia and Yeltsin, yet 15 different entities have arisen from the old Soviet Union. Have you had a chance to observe the quality and capabilities of the leadership of all 15 republics?

MR. LANDIS: I have not studied that area, though I am generally aware that they are all former Communists.

I think the West can identify with the Baltic states. They were Western-oriented until they were taken over in World War II, and they do know what capitalism is about. They have good relations with Scandinavia, Britain, and continental Europe. Prospects are quite good there, even though the possibility always exists that they won't be economically viable.

The remainder of the republics, as far as I can tell, are led by Communists, and that situation doesn't mean that, like Yeltsin, they cannot gradually do the job. I'm optimistic about all of them, frankly.

COMMENT: American experts' reactions to what happens in the old Soviet Union seem to be in constant flux. The United States has gone from the notion of the ten-foot-tall Russian to the "Chicken Little" syndrome. It took 70 years to erode the Slavic world there, and now the United States is expecting everything to change in a couple of years.

I had the good fortune of spending five years in the Soviet Union. I traveled five months out of the year and sat at the table with Khrushchev, Kosygin, Mikoyan, and others. During the Berlin crisis Averell Harriman came into town, and the ambassador had a luncheon and invited the hierarchy, including Khrushchev, who had a great sense of humor. At the close of the luncheon, which was a rather relaxed affair, Harriman said to Khrushchev, "Mr. Prime Minister, I like the dacha where I am staying. Give it to me and I will come in and be your adviser." Khrushchev smiled and said, "It's yours, but I don't have to take your advice." Then Khrushchev said, "Allow me to tell an anti-Soviet joke," and proceeded to tell it. So there was a sense of humor, and as you say, a great admiration for Americans. After traveling with 16 delegations, they used to refer to me as one of themselves, because there were people with whom I often met and traveled.

I think the American people really don't appreciate the Soviets like the people who operated in the Soviet hinterland. There was constantly a conspiracy there against the government. They just expressed it differently. In the old days they were able to conspire against the government. Now they don't have a government to conspire against. This situation sort of disarms them. Some of the farm managers were sharp people. One could sit and talk to them, and they would relate the details of Soviet politics.

I think the United States could have predicted what would happen to the Soviet Union if someone had gone back and read the records of the reports the American embassy had sent in. I myself had sent in reports every week on the food situation, production, and other related issues. The United States had a lot of information. Those who dared to say anything pointed out that

American experts coming to the Soviet Union were like people going to see a dog dance. They were so impressed by the fact that the dog got on its hind legs they failed to notice that it wasn't really dancing! We pointed this out in our reports, but in Washington when they wanted information on the Soviet Union, they didn't go to the people in the field; they brought in experts from Harvard or Yale. This situation is one of the things I think people have to consider in the current ferment.

MR. LANDIS: I think there is no question about that. Also, as you mentioned, the embassy and its experts are very important. The United States had terrific representation with Jack Matlock as the ambassador for the last eight or ten years. He is now back in the United States. The United States does not have a Russian-trained ambassador in Moscow. When it is so important to understand who the players are, who the players are going to be, and what the trends are among the people, the United States needs an expert.

To some extent the academic world has to take a hard look at the whole question of political science theory where it tends to optimistically categorize lots of countries in the same way, based on the notion that all countries have much in common. I think the cultural effects of different countries on their governments' policies have to be reemphasized.

I'm no expert on Japan, but it provides another example of the gap between U.S. knowledge and cultural realities. Is the training American universities are providing emphasizing enough the cultural differences and the effects those cultural differences have on the policies and stability of foreign governments?

QUESTION: Is the Russian mind capable of dealing with the country's non-Russian population without resorting to violence?

MR. LANDIS: When I speak about the Russian mind, there is a disturbing aspect here that I didn't emphasize, but perhaps it is between the lines: the appreciation for order and the lack of patience with dissenters. Nationalism comes into play as one starts talking about the Russian mind versus the Ukrainian's or

Belarussian's and so forth. There is a large Russian minority in the Ukraine, also a serious potential problem.

Russians are not very tolerant of minorities. A good article in the *Wall Street Journal* yesterday described the great difficulties of the Russians who are in Latvia. They are having a tough time because they are not welcome back in Moscow since they are Latvian Russians. They are not wanted in Latvia because they are Russians. Many of them are prominent individuals in Latvian society because Russians have long dominated Latvia.

QUESTION: Over the years it is the things the United States *hasn't* done as a nation that I find most disturbing. By its inaction, the United States joined in the forcible repatriation of the Russian prisoners of war who were immediately slaughtered by Stalin; the United States stood by—except for the brilliant air end run during the Berlin blockade—watching the Wall being built; the United States stood by when the Soviets crushed rebellions in Czechoslovakia and Hungary. Do you think a more active policy would have been a sounder policy?

MR. LANDIS: I would not presume to say that U.S. policy could have been different. What I mean to emphasize are Soviet perceptions and how important they are in the continuing rivalry.

I don't know that Truman had any choice as to whether he could have rattled the bomb and gotten results during the Berlin Crisis. Still, it probably would not have been a good idea.

The later cases, particularly during the Eisenhower years, were sad in the sense that the United States did so much, but still so little. On the positive side, the United States built up Radio Free Europe, and in so doing, the message to the Eastern Europeans was "We are behind you." It built up their expectations greatly for the Hungarian revolution.

I have been impressed by emigre professors in that regard. Jan Karski, a brilliant professor at Georgetown University, was in the underground in Poland. He felt that building up the hopes of Eastern Europeans and then not having any program for real change was a grave mistake. The fact that Khrushchev waited for ten days or two weeks before deciding to move the troops back into

Hungary *en masse* indicates that there was indecision in the Soviet Union.

I wouldn't say that U.S. policies could have or should have been different in respect to confronting the Soviets. I don't mean to be partisan here in any sense, but it struck me after the intervention in Czechoslovakia that rather than being tough with them in the aftermath, President Johnson was the lame duck and he instead sought to get a summit meeting going. In a way, this move was recognizing Soviet legitimacy despite their military intervention in Czechoslovakia. It might be useful to study some of these Western policies or attitudes and see to what extent the West might have unnecessarily helped the Soviet system stabilize itself and stave off its collapse.

COMMENT: I have a few thoughts on Eastern Europe. The United States stood by, as you mentioned, while uprisings in Berlin, Czechoslovakia, and Hungary raged. I don't know so much about President Eisenhower, but Secretary of State Dulles seemed to be so preoccupied with the Suez business that the real crisis was missed. I think Dulles's policy of brinkmanship was far too rigid. He also removed Chip Bohlen from his role as ambassador, which was unfortunate. I am not surprised that the United States was frozen into that kind of blind policy with Dulles. Why didn't Eisenhower pick someone far better? Four opportunities arose for a different approach: Berlin, the Czechs, the Hungarians, and the Poles. On top of that, Dulles's policy alienated the French for a generation.

QUESTION: You may have seen an article in the *Washington Post* this morning reporting an angry speech by Lech Walesa in Stuttgart saying how much the Polish people resent the activities of foreign capitalists in Poland. A danger exists that Poland will revert to a directed economy. Do you think this danger extends across the Eastern European countries and the former Soviet Union republics?

MR. LANDIS: I would think that all of the Eastern European countries are going to have a very difficult time retrofitting their economies. Certainly the republics within the former Soviet Union face the greatest difficulties because they haven't had, except in the Baltic countries, the tradition of experience with free-market capitalism.

I have heard, for example, a Polish intellectual tell about how the outlook is very bleak in Poland. He did not understand how within a short number of years a country could develop a multiparty system. There is no real foundation for it.

Everyone is aware of Russia's unfamiliarity with capitalism. They don't know whether they like or dislike capitalism based on what they have seen. They have heard so much rhetoric about various things that they can't make a fair judgment. In fact, they are getting their fill now when they go to stores and the prices are so high. If this is an example of the free market, they don't like it.

Is the present procedure for converting to a free market a sound one in Russia? It is hard to say. I'm not an economist, but it seems to me that they cannot continue to have major industries—energy and heavy industry—under government control. The success of the economy and the GNP from year to year may depend on how heavy industry is handled, even though in other areas they are moving toward private enterprise.

Certainly the small agricultural plot owner in the past has done a great deal to bolster the Soviet economy by proportionately feeding many more people than the big state farms. It is hard to believe, however, that a little capitalism, even accompanied by a lot of optimism, will bring the free market much success soon. This uncertainty extends to all of Eastern Europe.

COMMENT: Two days ago a U.S. embassy was opened in Kazakhstan, and within the next day or two a new ambassador will be named to Ukraine. Meanwhile, the U.S. embassy in Russia has relaxed the restrictions in place for 45 years that prohibited American nationals from mingling unaccompanied with the natives. Under Ambassador Robert Strauss, many people think the rapport with the Russians, which you mentioned as a strength, will increase.

Regarding Ambassador Strauss, I was also perplexed as to why the United States would send a man who is not an expert on the Soviet political system. I talked to a few professors about Jack Matlock's replacement, and Matlock was certainly an expert in this area. It seems the choice was based on Ambassador Strauss's alignment with the Democrats.

I also wonder why a Republican president would choose a Democratic party leader. As a young student of Soviet politics, it didn't strike me as terribly rational, but evidently Ambassador Strauss is known as a dealmaker, a people person, and a streetwise businessman. Perhaps U.S. policy is looking toward making these future business connections, and Strauss can help.

MR. LANDIS: I think when he was appointed, the outlook seemed to be fairly certain that the main thrust of U.S. policy would be economic. That appointment occurred before the Commonwealth was established, so perhaps there was a lot of validity to appointing him at that time. Most important, the United States needs to be closely in contact with the people themselves. That contact doesn't necessarily require a business or political background.

NARRATOR: Symbolically, one of our finest graduate students has asked a practitioner, in a sense, as well as a scholar a final question. I thought that in much of what you said there was common ground shared by scholars and practitioners. Yet, there always seems to be this divorce between those who study politics and those who practice it, between theory and practice, if you will. One of the purposes of the Miller Center is to try to close that gap. Thanks to Betsy and John Wright, who made this visit possible, we feel we have taken a step in that direction.

CHAPTER THREE

Change and the Continuing Revolution in the Soviet Union*

WALTER SABLINSKY, NATALIE KONONENKO, AND SANDRA GUBIN

NARRATOR: We are here today to refute the proposition that prophets are not without honor save in their own country. We have three prophets from the University of Virginia who will try to penetrate the mystery of an enigma wrapped in a riddle that is the Soviet policy. We are honored that three such leading scholars in the field of Soviet and Slavic studies would join us.

Professor Sablinsky was born in Russia, grew up in China, received his doctorate at the University of California-Berkeley, and offers major courses on Russian and Soviet history in the history department. He also has been a leader in the Center for Russian and East European Studies at the University.

Natalie Kononenko has her doctorate from Harvard University. She is a member of the faculty of Slavic languages and literature. She is an expert on folklore and Ukraine.

Sandra Gubin received her doctorate from the University of Michigan. She offers courses in the Department of Government and Foreign Affairs on Soviet government and politics.

We will begin with Professor Sablinsky followed by Professors Kononenko and Gubin to invite their different perspectives on today's topic.

Presented in a Forum at the Miller Center of Public Affairs on 17 October 1991.

MR. SABLINSKY: It is a very difficult time to speak about Russia because the whole thing is in such a state of flux that I don't think they know themselves what is happening. I am reminded of a quote by Peter the Great, who said, "Things that do not happen, happen in Russia."

We literally do not know the structure of the governments now. It is very difficult to perceive the leadership. Some people are recognizable, but how much power they will wield, no one knows. The strongest person that came out of the coup attempt is Boris Yeltsin. He is highly respected, almost loved, in Russia. He is by far the most prominent person, but is unsure of his own position. I recently read an article about archives of the Communist party being forwarded to one of the think tanks in Washington because Yeltsin himself doesn't know how long he will be in office.

Gorbachev's position is a bit weaker, but generally Gorbachev has a great deal of name recognition outside of the Soviet Union. He is much more popular outside of Russia than he is in Russia, where he is perceived essentially as a reluctant reformer.

Gorbachev began as leader of the Communist party in 1985. He wanted to reform the economy that was floundering and falling apart in order to preserve the Communist party's power. He remained such until the very end. Even after the coup, he was defending the Communist party. He surrounded himself with thugs, to put it frankly. It was an unsavory group, the people who carried out that coup. They did it with the help of his people, so therefore much of the blame goes to him.

I wonder when he started in 1985 if he would have done what he did had he known what was going to happen. What he did was dismantle the Communist party. He dismantled the structure, for which people are grateful. But was this dismantling intentional or not?

What impresses me about Yeltsin is that his position was very clear from the beginning. Once he took the side of the reform, he faced the party, eventually walking out of the party. He was elected by Russians.

Again, an important thing about him was that he surrounded himself with credible people. Almost everyone who could be looked upon from a positive point of view came over to his side—people

36

like Shevardnadze, Yakovlev, Silayev, Subchek of St. Petersburg, Popov of Moscow—all credible people.

The problem with Yeltsin was a certain distrust of him because he comes out of a culture that really admires the authoritarian approach. After all, he is nothing but a Communist boss. Again, however, during the coup and after the coup he proved to be consistent in the selection of people. For example, he objected to the selection of Moiseev for the head of the military. He was instrumental in some of the crucial appointments made by Gorbachev after the coup.

Again, I am impressed by Yeltsin's sensitivity towards various national issues. After the coup, he acted in a very statesmanlike manner, and I hope this will continue. Russia is facing enormous problems, with economic problems being number one. The economy is in shambles. Looking at the statistics of the decrease in production, one wonders if they are going to have enough food. I think they will, but the big cities will suffer. The countryside and the peasants will do all right.

The nationality problem is enormous, and Yeltsin has not really faced that issue yet. There are 25 million Russians who live outside of Russia. When the boundaries of the republics were drawn, they were drawn very artificially, because after all, everyone knew where the power was, so whether this nationality or that nationality received a little bit more, it didn't make much difference. Meanwhile the Russians were simply colonizing and settling whole areas in Ukraine, for example, that are now Russian enclaves. Out of a population of 52 million in Ukraine, over 10 million are Russians, mostly living in the eastern and southern parts of the republic. Crimea and cities like Odessa are entirely Russian.

The same is true of Kazakhstan. In Kazakhstan there are as many Russians as there are Kazakhs. Probably more people speak Russian than Kazakh. Think of how difficult it is going to be to try to separate all of those ethnic groups.

It is the same in the Baltic countries. In Estonia, the Estonians are in a minority, as are Latvians in Latvia. The Lithuanians are better off; there are about 20 percent that are not Lithuanian. This problem is going to be enormous. From the Russian point of view, wherever one looks, it appears disastrous.

From a historian's point of view, whenever Russians faced that kind of situation in the past, they always resorted to authority. Again and again, when one looks at Russian history going back to the 16th century, whenever a breakdown of authority occurs, there is turmoil and chaos. Chaos prevailed in the beginning of the 17th century in a period called the Time of Troubles. The dynasty broke down, and everyone was at each other's throat, so they got together and reestablished absolutism as the only way to keep things under control.

The same thing happened in 1917. Again, it was a breakdown of authority, and again autocracy fell, but the Communist party was reestablished with an authoritarian state.

The same thing is happening now. I am afraid from a historical point of view that if anything begins to break down, the logical escape would be a return to an authoritarian structure in order to keep things together.

Let me end by telling an old Russian joke. It is about God, who decided to answer some of the questions that departed leaders had for him. The first one was Mao Zedong, who asked, "What will happen to China?" God answered, "China will become capitalist." Mao Zedong turned away and began to cry. Then Truman asked, "What will happen to the United States?" God answered, "America will become socialist." So Truman shed some tears. When Brezhnev asked, "Comrade God, what will happen to the Soviet Union?" God didn't say anything. He turned away and began to cry.

MS. KONONENKO: My subject is Ukraine. Ukraine is not only a large and important country to the Soviet Union, or whatever is left of the Soviet Union, but many interesting developments are taking place there.

I will relate some of my personal experiences and then use them to discuss a phenomenon that is important to Ukraine and some of the other republics as well: the *diaspora*. I think the republics that have a *diaspora* have a different level of self-awareness than other Soviet states. They have a firmer sense of national, as opposed to Soviet, identity and are much more independent and independence-minded. The two incidents I would like to take from my personal experience happened a year ago when I was at the First International Congress of Ukrainianists in Kiev.

This was a very exciting, emotional period; it was the first time some of the participants had a chance to visit Ukraine. For those of us who had worked there before, it was the first time that people helped us rather than the opposite. For the Ukrainian hosts, it was a time of great pride because they were hosting a congress that had Americans, Europeans, Australians, and people from the other Soviet republics. Blue and yellow Ukrainian national flags and embroidered blouses were everywhere. One could not really wear an embroidered blouse prior to about 1990 because it was considered a sign of nationalism. People wore crosses. Members of Rukh, the opposition political party, greeted members of the congress everywhere we went. At the opening session, there was a performance by artists who sang "Shche ne vmerla Ukraina," which is a national anthem, a song of resistance, and the audience sang with them.

For me, personally, it was an emotional time because I learned that my grandfather (various things had happened to my grandfather, more than I can tell here) had been rehabilitated, exactly 100 years to the month after his birth. His books were on display at the Academy of Sciences, and I learned about his rehabilitation from a young man who was writing a book about him.

I was very excited. I got on a bus with Western colleagues to travel from the hotel to the meeting site, and I said, "You should all be very pleased. You now no longer have to ride on the bus with a descendant of an enemy of the people." The man sitting next to me said, "As a matter of fact, the Soviets would do well to blow up this entire bus, because we are all either enemies of the people or descendants of enemies of the people." That was incident number one.

Incident number two occurred while I was attending a session at the congress. A woman asked me about an American colleague. She made a point of attending my talk and then gave me a book about the political importance of the Ukrainian language. She followed me around, telling me how wonderful it was that I speak Ukrainian and study Ukrainian subject matter. I was flattered, but at the same time I was embarrassed by all of this adulation.

These incidents made sense much later in a less emotional situation and in combination with other things that had happened to me in the Soviet Union. I understood that many people who study Ukraine in the United States are themselves Ukrainian. They are often people who were either forced to leave Ukraine themselves or the descendants of such people. The official Soviet feeling about these people is one of tremendous antagonism. They are assumed to be anti-Soviet, raving Ukrainian nationalists, and ready to foment dissent at the drop of a hat.

These do not happen to be my feelings, but I cannot count the number of times that they were attributed to me. At this point, people who study the republics as opposed to people who study Russian topics should be distinguished because the tendency in assessing people who study the Russian republic is not to assume this great amount of nationalism. In fact, there is a tendency to assume naiveté, especially if people are not Russian descendants, whereas if one studies something in the republics, even if one is not Ukrainian, one is assumed to have been subverted to the Ukrainian point of view. That person is assumed to be a raving nationalist.

What this woman showed me is that while official attitudes view the emigres as enemies, the people's attitude is diametrically the opposite. The people in the *diaspora* are assumed to be wonderful. They are the emblem of all that is good and true. If a true Ukrainian language exists, it is preserved abroad, in Canada more than in the United States. If true Ukrainian culture, literature, art, and history exists, They are, again, abroad.

It is assumed that Ukrainians abroad will lead their homeland to freedom and salvation. In fact, this term, the *diaspora*, is something that has come into use quite recently, and it does assume that people will return with this agenda of salvation. The amount of time that Ukrainian political leaders spend abroad is really noteworthy, and they are in contact with Ukrainian-Americans, particularly American scholars of Ukrainian descent.

Many Ukrainian leaders have visited the *diaspora* in the United States. When Ukrainian President Leonid Kravchuk visited the United Nations and President Bush, he also went to the Harvard Ukrainian Research Institute. Drach, the head of Rukh, and Dziuba attended the Ukrainian Seminar at the University of

Illinois last summer. Solomya Pavlychko, head of the Ukrainian women's movement, has also visited the United States. Many, many Ukrainian political leaders have had discussions with the Ukrainian *diaspora* here in the United States.

There is nothing comparable in Russia. I do not see Gorbachev talking to emigre Russians' sons or daughters. Solzhenitsyn keeps trying to give Gorbachev advice, but everyone knows what happens. Even Yeltsin is not turning to the emigres.

(I should mention briefly that among the Russian populace there is some interest in the emigres. I recently heard a nostalgic talk about Nabokov. But even here there is a difference between the Russian situation and the Ukrainian one. There is a nostalgia for Nabokov as a representative of something finer that was lost. Unlike the Ukrainian emigres, Nabokov is not seen to embody the essence of Russian culture.)

The Ukrainian *diaspora*, on the other hand, is believed to embody true Ukrainian culture. For Soviet Ukrainians, the *diaspora* is a kind of safe-deposit box. In it Ukrainian culture is preserved and its existence gives them a sense of identity and confidence that they will survive until economic and political independence are achieved. Extrapolating from the Ukrainian situation, I think that this feeling might be true of the other republics that have a sizable *diaspora*.

I have talked about perception. Let me say a few words about reality. The *diaspora* is not what Soviet Ukrainians perceive it to be. Most of the *diaspora* does not even call itself that. They see themselves as ethnics rather than emigres. They are Ukrainian-Americans or Ukrainian-Canadians, with an emphasis on the noun rather than the adjective. They would like to visit Ukraine on vacation, but they do not want to return there for good; neither do they want to liberate anything.

These Ukrainians have assimilated to the West. Their language has adopted anglicisms. They have developed a New York school of Ukrainian poetry that borrows English language metaphors and reflects its New York environment. In the States, people make the emblem of Ukrainian nationhood, the Easter egg, using Western tools and dyes. They use ostrich eggs. Those embroidered shirts I mentioned earlier as another national emblem are made of polyester. Assimilation is everywhere. Quiche, by the way, has become part of the Christmas Eve meal.

What will happen with increased contact between the West and Soviet Ukrainians? What will happen when the Ukrainians find out that the *diaspora* is not what they think it is? Obviously, there will be some disappointment.

To give an example of disappointment I myself saw: In my visits to Ukraine, I was asked to lend assistance. People would give me voluminous manuscript series and ask that I take them back to the United States to be published. These people had helped me, and I wanted to help them in return. It was difficult to explain that the manuscripts might not be published. They would say, "I can't publish this here; Soviet authorities will cut it." I hated to tell them that such manuscripts would be cut in the West as well, if published at all, though not for political reasons.

On another occasion, some people handed me Ukrainian blouses and said, "Take these to the United States, sell them for $200 or $300, and buy us a VCR." Again, Ukrainian blouses may be a hot item in Ukraine, but I'm not sure they would fetch hundreds of dollars here. Most Ukrainian-Americans prefer T-shirts that say, "Kiss me, I'm Ukrainian" or "Do it with a *bandura*," as anyone can verify by attending the Ukrainian festival in New Jersey.

What impact will all of this have on Ukraine? The young will surely simply adopt Western, T-shirted Ukrainianism. How about their elders and, more important, how about political impact?

For a long time I have been afraid that disappointment with the *diaspora* might be one disappointment too many. As many people know, perestroika (perebudova in Ukrainian) has restructured nothing. I was afraid that disappointment with the *diaspora*, on top of political and economic disappointment, might be more than the Ukrainians could take and that it would have a negative effect on Ukraine's drive toward independence. Instead, the drive is strong and powerful. The strength of Ukrainian feeling is phenomenal. Russian-speakers in Donetsk are calling themselves Ukrainians, learning the Ukrainian language and working for Ukrainian independence. The drive for independence is overcoming age-old factionalism. Old Catholic-Orthodox differences, for example, have been put aside in favor of the Ukrainian cause.

In fact, if any disunity is threatening the Ukrainian cause, it is among the *diaspora*. Among Ukrainian-Americans and Ukrainian-Canadians, a split has long existed between political refugees and economic refugees. This split exists for socioeconomic reasons, the political and the economic refugees coming from different social strata. This split also exists because political refugees feel they were punished precisely by being expelled from Ukraine and that the willingness of others to leave the homeland devalues the pain and longing they felt as a result of expulsion. More important, disunity exists among the *diaspora* now because there is a struggle for power. Ukrainian-Americans and Ukrainian-Canadians clearly feel that whoever is in charge in the *diaspora* will have a tremendous and lasting impact on the future of Ukraine. Power on this side of the Atlantic implies power on the other, and there has been a great deal of fighting. For the sake of my homeland, I hope it stays on this side of the Atlantic.

MS. GUBIN: I believe there are two possible scenarios of what is likely to happen in the Soviet Union in the aftermath of the coup. Since Professor Sablinsky was a little pessimistic, I am going to lean toward the optimistic interpretation today.

There is no doubt that the coup gave impetus to the reform process. Indeed, Alexander Yakovlev is quoted as saying he thinks they should give the Gang of Eight medals. This quote created a gasp among the Soviets, but he is right in the sense that the coup provided new impetus for the reform process.

What people have seen since then, however, is what they have seen for the past six years in the Soviet Union: a not surprising lack of consensus about how to proceed into the future. There has repeatedly been a lot of agreement about what people don't want or what they are against, but very little as to what that means about moving into the future. While I do not think Gorbachev intended for the reforms to be as radical as they have become, I do think that over the years he has tried to build consensus gradually over time to move forward. Obviously at times, I think he has moved too slowly, but he has taken an approach of attempting to build consensus.

What people see now in terms of these problems is best exemplified in all of the reports coming out about the new economic union treaty. It calls for having a central bank, a single currency, and a free flow of trade. People barely had time to read these reports before the Ukrainian and Russian republics began backing off from the agreements. They continue to take a more protectionist stance. As part of this process everyone wants to protect himself, not surprisingly, from the center that has done so much harm.

Underneath all of this is contradiction. I always tell my students that to study Soviet politics is to study contradictions. Every society has its contradictions, but this country has turned it into an art form. What everyone is seeing now is the continued expression of this contradiction. On one hand, the republics recognize that this economy is terribly interdependent and that the center does have a role in coordinating things. On the other hand, not surprisingly, the republics are very distrustful of the center and are trying to build up themselves and take for themselves what they can get.

Adding to this problem is Russia's protectionism. This protectionism is based on its fear of exploitation by the periphery because it is the largest republic with the most natural resources. At the same time, indications from Yeltsin and others suggest that they still see themselves in the dominant leadership role in whatever the future is for the former Soviet Union. The republics react because they fear Russia is playing too dominant a role. What they are trying to do is come out and balance this.

The determining factor may actually be the outside world, because in fact the West is basically saying, "You all have to decide on some kind of uniform agreement to move into the future before we are going to invest and help you out." Not long ago, I would have said that the West's influence on this process is marginal. However, as the economy continues to deteriorate and they are pushed into having to cope with this problem, there is a way in which the West is having greater influence on what direction they

44

will take. I do think that one sees both selfishness and realism constantly in conflict, but that the process continues to go on.

So my optimistic scenario for the Soviet Union is that, just as for the past six years in which people have seen a process that has continued to go forward and have said, "This is the breaking point," the former Soviet Union will continue to go forward. Many people have said, "This is it! They will never get rid of the leading role of the Communist party. When it moves to that, we are going to go backwards." Analysts have always seen the potential, which is still there, for a move back to a more authoritarian society. Nevertheless, taking two steps forward, sometimes three steps back and sometimes only one step back, the process has continued to expand at a most remarkable rate for six years. Violence has occurred, but given a country that has an extraordinarily violent history, the fact that so little violence has occurred in this process is nothing short of remarkable. Not enough attention, in my opinion, is paid to that aspect.

What will be seen in the future will be the same kind of two steps forward, three steps back, two steps forward, one step back; nevertheless, there will be forward progress. There will be, as is evident in all of the hesitation and attempts to protect themselves, some recognition that the center is important in this process for the time being. Remember that this society has been deliberately economically segregated so that they are terribly interdependent. Until each of the republics can become more self-sufficient, the center still has a role in coordination.

In this process, while Yeltsin is the man of the moment according to today's *New York Times*, he has been very hesitant about actually implementing economic reform procedures. His popularity is declining because people are judging all of the leaders on what they produce, and the situation isn't getting any better under Yeltsin than it had been under Gorbachev.

In this process, I believe that Gorbachev, while not as powerful as he was, still has a role to play as the consensus builder and to some degree in helping to keep the balance of the republics—surprisingly, given the fact that he didn't understand the nationality issue—against the rising power of Russia; that is, Yeltsin. So, Gorbachev is still an actor in this process.

45

I can't exactly predict the future, but my feeling is that they have set the base, they have struggled forward, and with fits and starts, they will continue to move into a more democratic future. The process will continue.

My pessimistic scenario is that one cannot ignore Russian history, and that periods of reform have always been followed by periods of oppression. There is continuing ethnic conflict and frustration with the enormous amount of anarchy in the former Soviet Union, although it has been tolerated to a greater degree than our understanding of political culture would have led us to believe. If the shortages become severe—and again, people don't have any good sense of how much the shortages are due to a breakdown in the distribution system rather than the actual production system—and the leadership fails to actually implement reforms that will produce some optimism for the future, this failure will indeed create the situation for another coup. Even then, however, I believe that it might be a coup in line with the kind of military coups that have taken place in Latin America. The military, with other political forces—and this is the point where I always stick my neck out—in combination with Boris Yeltsin, who would give them legitimacy, could take over under the guise of restoring order. Even in this scenario, while it will be a more authoritarian system, the Soviet Union will still move toward greater, if slower, marketization of the economy and will recognize some fundamental human rights within it, although undoubtedly freedom of press will not be among them.

I am arguing that one cannot go back to Brezhnev. This is still a process of modernization, and the military, combined with others, will continue to modernize. This is a process of having to redo what they failed to do to some degree during the past 70 years. If they are going to modernize, they are going to have to move forward with some level of marketization and decentralization, although this scenario would imply doing it at a much slower pace and with more oppression.

COMMENT: Thus far, the focus has been mostly on urban activities. However, slightly less than half of the total population of the Soviet Union is rural and is distributed over 50,000 state and

46

collective farms. Each is a fiefdom unto itself, with the chairman in authority either at times cooperating with or conspiring against the central government. The units are somewhat stable. In many cases the chairman is a Communist hack, but in many others they have built up a rapport with their constituents that range up to 500 families in some of the larger units.

These rural units are a conservative but stable element in the structure at the present time. Very little has been said about events there or if in fact what is happening or what will happen is comparable to what is going on in Czechoslovakia, which is moving much faster. There the collective farms have become cooperatives; the people have now chosen to retain what has been. The collective farm is now a cooperative, and those who want to stay operate the farm.

An important thing that will be happening in the Soviet Union will be the activity that is taking place in the rural areas. They have been very active in the past as far as conspiracy goes. I have visited many of the farms where they could communicate with their eyes when one of the authorities was present. Some of these farms are so remote that their only connection with central authority is by telephone, so they are largely operating their own system.

People read in the newspapers during the wintertime about livestock dying as a result of murrain. The murrain was actually internal slaughter for their own tables. I think some attention needs to be paid to the rural countryside to see what is actually going to happen in the Soviet Union.

MS. KONONENKO: Even a year ago there was already a great deal of private entrepreneurship, where people were selling buckets of plums, pears, and potatoes on the main street in Kiev. They were already trying to make a switch, and they were quite actively and successfully selling by the road.

MR. SABLINSKY: I think agriculture is probably more important than industry. If anything is going to happen in Russia, it will have to be on the agrarian level.

The problem is that Russia is run on bureaucracy. Approximately 18 million bureaucrats are running Russia, with approxi-

47

mately four million running agriculture alone. Bureaucrats don't produce many crops, but how does one remove them and pass the land to the peasants so it can be worked by peasants?

When property was collectivized, peasants were given an opportunity to retain what they called a household plot. It is a half acre around their house. That 2 percent of the land held by peasants produces more than half of all of the vegetables in Russia. It also produces two-thirds of all of the eggs and half of the poultry. They had to do it because they could not have fed the country otherwise.

In visiting the collective farms, one is struck by the brown color everywhere and the green color around the houses. If it is an intensive type of agriculture, things grow around the houses and do not in the fields. In some ways one could say that probably the best thing that could be done is to simply double or triple the amount of land a peasant can have, but that action goes against the system. It is a collective farm, and there also is vested interest in the people who run the collective farm to retain that field.

When peasants are given private land, they get the worst land. They get land in unaccessible areas, and there is a great deal of resentment on the part of authorities. In other words, if a peasant wants land, he wants to be a capitalist. In the long run it will be a lengthy, gradual process to reeducate the people and change their attitudes. How can capitalism be promoted in a country in which capitalism is a bad word? How can entrepreneurship be encouraged where no one has it? How can a system of incentives be created? By the way, Russians don't even have a word for incentive. What they need is a system of incentives that will reward production, especially in agriculture. That is the biggest problem they are going to face.

QUESTION: About nuclear power—according to a recent article in *Time*, if the nuclear power is distributed to the new republics, Ukraine and Belarus will be the third and fourth leading nuclear countries. Apparently there is some hesitation about getting rid of all of these facilities. Could you comment on the impact of nuclear power on the changes in the Soviet Union and the anticipated and possible authoritarian regression?

MS. GUBIN: I think this is an area in which they are between a rock and a hard place in some sense, and they recognize it. This area will have more impact on the degree to which they become separate and their attitudes toward separatism than the authoritarian issue. If Ukraine, given the most recent fire in Chernobyl, wants to get rid of nuclear power, they will become even more dependent on Russian oil. On their own, they are going to have to continue operating Chernobyl. So, I think its implication is much more for the continued union than it is for the issue of authoritarianism, and what people are going to see is a continued fight in the former Soviet Union on all environmental issues, not just the nuclear issue.

Where is the trade-off? The West is at a point in its development where it can now begin to talk about the trade-offs between the costs of development and preservation of the environment, and there still are problems in the United States with this area. They are in a position where their industrialization process has left them, at minimum, 40 years behind where the United States is. The exploitation of the environment for development continues to be an issue in light of the existing pollution problem. They haven't dealt with it, even beginning at the level the West has, whatever its problems. This is a horrible set of trade-offs to make, and I don't think there are any easy solutions. I think they will gradually begin to look for solutions, and again, look toward the West for investment and technology, the technology of cutting it down.

MS. KONONENKO: Chernobyl was a point that turned Ukrainian consciousness toward Ukrainian nationalism in Ukraine. The degree to which they seem to see that as a catalyst around which everyone rallies I can't understand, and probably few people in the West can understand. As for weapons, many may have heard Ukraine was going to be a nuclear-free zone. Now they are changing their mind.

QUESTION: In talking about the possible increase and importance of the impact of outside influence, isn't it true that the United States also has some confusion in the outside realm with respect to

49

the Soviet Union not only because of their problems and the difficulty of knowing with whom to negotiate on a contract but also because American priorities are difficult to arrive at? The United States has discovered that it cannot very well tell people how to make a quick transition from a highly centralized bureaucratic society to a full-blown market economy, so it advises on the periphery of it.

I wonder in this connection if this country could provide more assistance to the Soviet republics if it concentrated particularly on the technologies that Americans have a mastery of, such as distribution and consumption machinery. Americans could help bypass some of the bureaucracies, since bureaucracies seldom disintegrate themselves, by helping them to set up new shortcuts around bureaucracy.

Americans should also recognize that much of the initiative in the Soviet Union, politically and economically, in the last six years has come from new leadership in the cities and elsewhere concerning local reforms around specific issues like environmental problems. This knowledge could be used to increase agricultural output with more peasant output, increase manufacturing so that peasants can buy something with their money, and increase manufacturing in the element of clothing and immediate consumer goods. A great deal could be done with the oil industry because recent Soviet prosperity was largely built on the development of its oil capacity. It is now dropping off drastically. It is very much in the interest of the United States to see it come back again.

MS. GUBIN: I would agree with you, and I think that certainly is the way the new American ambassador approaches relations with the Soviet Union. What he has said is that he is interested in small packages that have an impact over time, and I think that he defines his role as focusing on economic development and fostering deals.

What would be helpful is if the administration, in conjunction with Europe, could come up with some idea of plans that either had to do with regional economic development and/or specific areas of industry that would focus and encourage investment there. At that level I agree with you. I don't know that the administration has focused on developing a real policy.

COMMENT: An earlier comment was made comparing the equal rights under law of women and saying that they are the same in Russia. To get to the practical level, I think one has to take into account a very important factor, which is the difference in the number and availability of lawyers.

NARRATOR: What about lawyers in the Soviet Union?

MS. GUBIN: I don't think it is just the number of lawyers; I think it is the institution and the role of law. If a society isn't law-governed, the existence of a constitution and what is in the constitution borders on the irrelevant.

They do have advocates with the equivalent of a master's degree in law who someone can go to and pay a ruble. The problem in the Soviet Union has been that for any kind of complaint, every ministry has had its own set of secret laws and operating instructions to which the plaintiff's lawyer is denied access, so that the role of law in the Soviet Union has made the existence of constitutional guarantees almost irrelevant.

QUESTION: When the dust finally settles and they write the history of this era, do you think Gorbachev could be considered the father of his country or the originator of this movement?

MR. SABLINSKY: Well, he definitely gets the credit. He started the whole thing, but as I mentioned before, there seems to have been some reluctance on his part.

COMMENT: That is right now, but when the thing gets a rosy glow 20 or 30 years from now, he might become a George Washington or someone like that.

MR. SABLINSKY: Maybe not George Washington, but certainly a person who set the thing in motion; after all, he is associated with reforms, perestroika, and glasnost. Glasnost is successful; perestroika is not yet.

Political optimism is only associated with the coup. It is a kind of euphoria, and I am really surprised at this adulation of Yeltsin.

51

Russians are solidly behind him. I am afraid he might emerge as the leader of a Russian republic, which would be the dominant republic. Again, this is the problem. If one is a leader of a Russian republic and 25 million Russians are living outside of the republic, that situation creates all sorts of possibilities and problems. I think Gorbachev will be given his due.

QUESTION: Won't these Russians become Ukrainians, Estonians, or something else?

MS. KONONENKO: The ones in Ukraine are merrily becoming Ukrainians and are probably more nationalistic, sort of to prove themselves, than the ones with the -enko and the -chuk last names.

MR. SABLINSKY: In the Baltic countries, some people learn and speak the language, but the question is, are they going to be allowed to vote? There are others who live in enclaves and who are totally Russian and very nationalistic about Russia, especially in an area like Kazakhstan. The northern part of Kazakhstan is all Russian. The eastern part of Ukraine, Donetsk, and Dnepropetrovsk is almost all Russian.

MS. KONONENKO: The Rukh policy is that Russians will be permitted to vote and will be considered Ukrainian citizens.

MR. SABLINSKY: People aren't very far apart. They are all Slavs, and what separates them is the fact that they are under different domination. Ukraine started off being the center of Russia. That is where the word *Russia* comes from. But in the course of several centuries, Ukraine was occupied by Lithuania and Poland, and so was Belarus, the western part of Russia. So in the course of several centuries, they developed different languages, different cultures, and things of this sort. Many similarities exist, and the languages are not very far apart.

QUESTION: Would the progress of democratization in the erstwhile Soviet Union really contribute to the solution of fundamental economic problems? Isn't the Russian economy in a sort of chapter 11 condition where the control of the economy by the stockholders might not be to the best interest of everyone?

MS. GUBIN: Professor Gertrude Greenslade, a well-respected Soviet economist, says that there is no doubt that the Soviet economy is in serious difficulty, but people have this attitude of treating it like it's Burma. With all of its problems, it has tremendous natural resources; for all of the backwardness of its industrialization, it does have an industrial base. Throughout the last six years, they have laid the basis for some progress in terms of marketization, and it is there for them to act on.

Your question is well taken in the sense that it might proceed better if all of these political issues didn't exist and they would just focus on the economy. Many people see Yeltsin as a leader. One of the problems with Gorbachev is that he was too weak, and people see Yeltsin as a guy who is going to shove the reform down people's throats.

I still think that the loosening up of the politics has been important in driving this force forward. Whether or not at some point they could proceed better if someone were to stand up and say, "OK, we are just going to do it, and everyone is going to fall into line," remains to be seen. I think there is a tendency to think that is true, but it is almost an unanswerable question. If they were to have another coup and a more authoritarian regime, I think history shows that as it modernizes, the need for greater democratization will come, and even China, I think, is going to face that reality down the road.

NARRATOR: Should the United States give assistance to the Soviet Union? One school says—and I was raised in this school—that if it is in your country's national interest, regardless of the form of government, regardless of the economic system, that country ought to give assistance. Another view says that if they are not democratic and if they are not free enterprise, regardless of U.S. national interest, the United States shouldn't help them.

MS. GUBIN: I think the question has come down to something else. It is not a question of "Should the United States aid them."

It is, "How should the United States aid them?" I think it has to be done in a way that is not going to be just throwing money away because the United States doesn't have it to throw away anymore. Just propping things up could inhibit the reform process. So, the question is not whether we should aid them, but what form that aid should take.

NARRATOR: We are very grateful to our colleagues for this presentation. I think prophets sometimes are with honor in their own institution, and our speakers have all proved that to be true. Thank you.

II.

THE BALKAN EXPERIENCE

CHAPTER FOUR

Change in Eastern Europe*

DANIEL N. NELSON

NARRATOR: Daniel Nelson was born in Minneapolis. He graduated *summa cum laude* from the University of Minnesota in both history and political science. He received his master's and doctor's degrees from Johns Hopkins University.

He has taught in various places but has had a more permanent association with the University of Kentucky. During 1990, he was a senior associate at the Carnegie Endowment, and he has served as senior foreign policy adviser to the majority leader of the U.S. House of Representatives, Richard A. Gephardt. His bibliography attests to the areas about which he has written. His book, *The Balkan Imbroglio*, was published in 1991. He has also written several books and articles on Romanian politics in the Ceausescu era and elite-mass relations in communist systems.

Professor Nelson is a frequent television commentator and professional discussant on these issues. He joins this inquiry with a discussion of Eastern Europe in transition.

MR. NELSON: I propose to talk about several matters related to Eastern Europe. First, I want to discuss what has happened, and of course in doing that I will have to paint with a roller and not with a brush—it will be a broad portrait. Second, I want to discuss why some of these things have happened in Eastern Europe. Finally, I'll

---

Presented in a Forum at the Miller Center of Public Affairs on 1 October 1990.

prognosticate, or gaze into my crystal ball, since that is what those of us in think tanks are supposed to do.

Before beginning this discussion, I would like to preface it by telling a story. I was teaching a course on Soviet politics at the University of Kentucky in the fall of 1989. This was an auspicious time, even for teaching Soviet politics. I selected a textbook for this course in the spring of 1989, which is how professors select textbooks—a semester in advance. I ordered the textbook, and after it came in all of the students bought a copy. About the second or third day of class, I told the students to bring that textbook into the classroom with them. I then emulated the movie *Dead Poets' Society*, in which Robin Williams portrays a teacher who one day tells his students to rip out all of the pages of their textbook because he didn't like the way their textbook taught his subject. I told my students to open their Soviet textbook to page 21, which is where the historical section ended, and then to rip out all of the pages afterward. Some of the students looked a bit puzzled by this request, for they had just paid $19.95 for the book. I told them that they didn't actually have to rip these pages out but that they shouldn't read them because they were absolutely useless. In other words, I was teaching a course, and in the span of about six months, the textbook for that course had become ancient history. The textbook talked about the leading role of the Communist party of the Soviet Union. It talked about the absolute prohibition against autonomous organization. It described the stifling control of the KGB over society, the centralization of the economy, and all of those things. By late 1989 it was clear that all of these were unraveling fast. It is still unraveling, and it is not entirely gone, but the point is that I couldn't teach from that textbook.

Why do I tell this story? Partly to get a chuckle or two, but mostly to illustrate that the part of the world that I study is in an enormous and fundamental transformation that at least in the last couple of generations has been unequaled. That isn't to say that it is unprecedented in the scope of history. One can clearly recall other points in time when equal or greater transitions occurred. But this one *is* momentous.

At a very simplistic level, it is obvious that Communist parties were forced to retreat from positions of state authority. People have heard the term *revolution* used many times to reflect what happened from the Baltic to the Bosporus and from Poland through East Germany down to Sofia, Bulgaria. I suggest that the term *revolution* is probably misleading in terms of what happened in 1989 and 1990. One could say that what happened in 1989 was the culmination of a lengthy period of change, and therefore the term *silent revolution* might be better. That term isn't mine. It belongs to Ronald Englehart, a political scientist at the University of Michigan, who used the term in reference to Western Europe.

A silent revolution was going on during the 1970s and 1980s in Eastern Europe and to a degree in the Soviet Union itself. Some of this is revealed by public opinion data which, though not perfect, nevertheless provided incremental bits and pieces of information that indicated increasing antagonism towards these regimes. Some of this is revealed by organizational activity: Solidarity in Poland, Charter 77 in Czechoslovakia, the Lutheran Church in East Germany, and many others. Some of it is indicated by the incremental rise in the number of strikes and work stoppages. What I'm trying to say is that evidence was building that these systems ruled by Communist parties (let's not call them Marxist or Socialist parties) were incrementally losing their grip on political authority. I have written some pieces arguing that people were seeing a gradual rise of public legitimation and an expansion of nonsupportive participation during the 1970s and 1980s, and that 1989 was the point at which it reached the precipice and went over, albeit not at the same moment in all of the countries. While these Communist governments were still in control, they began to backpedal; they began to talk to opposition groups (in some countries) and to move away from an absolute rejection of any kind of responsiveness to public demands. Organizations were beginning to form that, if not desired by the authorities, were at least tolerated and not entirely outlawed. Communist party regimes were unraveling gradually, so 1989 then becomes not a revolution but a denouement—an end of the final stage in a revolutionary process.

If that is accepted as a general description of what happened, then the question should be, "What didn't happen?" In the United States people sometimes make mistakes in their assessments of what happened. I don't think that capitalism won and socialism lost.

I don't think what happened was that democracy won and some kind of Communist rule lost. I don't think what happened was that the United States won and the Soviet Union lost. I don't think there were necessarily those who won and those who were defeated. For many people the Cold War meant losses across the board.

That doesn't mean that there was no vindication of Western values. I am not suggesting that at all. Neither capitalism nor the United States, however, caused the fall of these regimes. What happened in 1989 was the culmination of a decade and a half or more of Communist systems that unraveled because of their own inherent weaknesses. What happened was the abject failure of a particular kind of system: a one-party, ideologically-driven, Leninist model. Communist rule did not work; it did not produce.

The courage and conviction of the people of Eastern Europe must be added to this failure. The real victors in this situation have been the people in Leipzig, Timisoara, Budapest, and Prague. To credit the demise of communism to NATO, the United States, or any particular American policy would be taking away the credit from where it is really due: the courageous people of Eastern Europe.

Why did all of this happen? One explanation of why these massive changes occurred in Eastern Europe (that are continued in the Soviet Union) is that Mikhail Gorbachev made it happen—that on his back and in his hands rests the transition that occurred after he assumed power in the Soviet Union in 1985. There is some truth to that statement. It was Gorbachev who ended what the United States had referred to as the Brezhnev Doctrine: the notion of limited sovereignty for the nations of Eastern Europe. It was he who decided not to intervene in Eastern Europe. However, I reject the great man theory of history as the principal cause and in a sense proximate reason for what happened in 1989 and 1990. Anyone who took over the role of general-secretary of the Communist party of the Soviet Union in 1985 would have had to have made significant changes. They should have been attempted earlier, but by 1985 these changes would have had to be made. Otherwise, there would have been a massive rebellion, far more violent and far more convulsive than any in Soviet history.

Not only did Gorbachev make these kinds of analyses, but many others long before him also saw the need for economic reform. There were the Liberman reforms during the Khrushchev period. There was Kosygin and his efforts at reform during the early years of the Kosygin-Brezhnev-Podgorny troika. The details of these earlier reforms are unimportant; what is important is that they represented an acknowledgement that the Soviet system needed reform. Therefore, I don't credit Gorbachev with causing all of this tumult that people have seen since 1985. At the very most, he acknowledged what was probably inevitable. If he didn't open the door, it was going to happen in a much more violent and convulsive way.

I do not think that U.S. foreign policy, per se, should be credited either. Bear in mind that by 1985 and 1986, because of U.S. budgetary deficits, the military buildup that was seen in the early Ronald Reagan presidency was beginning already to turn around. Therefore, if anyone tries to suggest that U.S. foreign policy is the proximate cause of this change, he or she is looking at something that had already begun to backtrack by 1986 or 1987, and certainly by 1988.

Internal causes are where one has to look for the explanation of events that took place in Eastern Europe and that are still taking place in the Soviet Union. To put it bluntly, people caused 1989 and 1990. Before that point, people, because of their attitudinal disaffection from these regimes, caused the unraveling of authoritarian rule and the transition to something else. People will recall the formation under duress of autonomous organizations, organizations that were born in the underground and gradually came above. There was Solidarity, which was outlawed in December 1981 but which continued its life underground; also, there was Charter 77. Others in other countries lived underground in difficult circumstances, even in Bulgaria and Romania. All of these organizations continued because of the courage and perseverance of individuals. I think this explanation is the most powerful one.

What were the motivations of the people? As I mentioned earlier, they were motivated not by external conditions but by the economic and political failures of these regimes. Under Communist

61

rule these countries did not provide what one political scientist has called "political goods." It was not only that the shop shelves were barren but also that basic fairness and equity were denied to the population. Also, the rule of law, that basic precept of any kind of legitimate authority, was lacking, and it was lacking by virtue of the antipathy of the population toward these regimes.

My first point is straightforward. One should look at what has happened in a different way: as a gradual process, and not just as the events of 1989 and 1990. Also, it is a process that is continuing. My second point is that one should look at these events as being caused not by something the United States did, by something one man did, or even by a victory of one nation over another, but rather by the failures of these systems and popular awareness of these failures.

What will the future hold for this part of the world? Everyone hopes that Eastern Europe and the Soviet Union, or parts of the Soviet Union, will eventually reach some form of democracy. People can debate about what democracy is or isn't, and I know of no clear-cut definition. Suffice it to say that a democratic government must engage in regularly scheduled elections, it must be responsive, and it must be characterized by the rule of law. These precepts are absolutely necessary. I have to say that in my judgment the prognosis is highly varied and not altogether good for some parts of Eastern Europe and some constituent parts of the Soviet Union.

There seem to be much stronger processes or much stronger sentiments other than a commitment to what Americans would call democratic precepts that are operating both in the countries of Eastern Europe and in the republics of the Soviet Union. Some of these sentiments are nationalistic. They are not necessarily linked to a particular ethnic group but are instead focused on the glorification of the strength of the state and nation. Some of the other powerful sentiments are rooted in ethnic identity, and when these two join, they form an ethno-nationalism that is a particularly volatile brew within Eastern Europe and the Soviet Union.

Some of the other motives that are stronger than democracy per se have a lot to do with economic subsistence. In countries like Poland, Romania, Bulgaria, and in regions of Yugoslavia and the

Soviet Union, economic subsistence is an issue because it is by no means guaranteed. For example, in some of these nations malnutrition and infant mortality are still vital issues. I just returned from Moscow and can guarantee that currently, not only is there a great deal of tension but also some desire that Gorbachev take emergency powers, almost dictatorial powers, in order to guarantee basic economic subsistence. Democracy is out the window, in a sense, if that rudimentary subsistence level is threatened.

While those on the outside desire democracy, and many of the people there desire it as well, factors intervene. For example, strength of nation, existence and protection of ethnic identity, language and culture, and economic subsistence are all issues in this part of Europe.

My opinions on several of the countries involved are as follows: Poland is certainly not guaranteed a democratic future. I wish I could say otherwise. Beginning in January, based upon a plan drafted by Jeffrey Sachs of Harvard University, Poland launched what I call "cold turkey" capitalism: Yesterday it was socialism, tomorrow, capitalism. The plan calls for a very rapid and wrenching reversal of the socioeconomic system from one of central planning and state ownership to one of no planning and private entrepreneurial activity. Thus far there is good news and bad news. Inflation is down, and there are things on the shelves. The reason why things are on the shelves, however, is because no one can afford them. Prices have risen enormously, and Poland is now in a deep recession. They are selling goods abroad, and their balance of trade has improved, but industrial output has fallen considerably while unemployment has risen.

Because of these present difficulties, Lech Walesa will now run for the presidency of Poland against the current prime minister, Tadeusz Mazowiecki, who is also a member of the Solidarity organization. Mazowiecki versus Walesa will further split Solidarity; it will leave it in shambles. I don't think that the prognosis for democracy is at all certain. Lech Walesa, as charming an individual as he is and as courageous, is a dubious prospect as president. He may win, but his notion of Polish foreign policy and domestic policy aren't clear or well formulated. Foreign policy for Poland will be an important issue in the future, for there are people to the far right, Polish nationalists, who claim land to Poland's east: Ukraine, Byelorussia, and Lithuania (the big Poland of 1610 to 1613). They could become volatile if they have any role in government.

Two days from now, what is presently East Germany will reunite with the Federal Republic. Therefore, its prognosis for democracy should be superb; yet one needs to wonder. I'm not trying to raise fears of Germany at all. What I am suggesting is that the eastern part of Germany is woefully unprepared (especially given such a short transition) to become part of the high-tech, high-priced world of western Germany. The twains are not going to meet for a long time. The people who have lived in the eastern part of Germany are going to suffer rather considerably from unemployment as their noncompetitive factories are shut down. Therefore, there is the possibility of unrest. Yes, there will still be a working democracy in a reunited Germany, but the transition period will be filled with tension.

In Czechoslovakia, the government of Vaclav Havel and Prime Minister Calfa is still on a honeymoon, but that honeymoon is wearing off. The world is already witnessing the beginnings of antagonisms between the Czechs and the Slovaks. Already the Slovaks have insisted on a hyphenated name for their country, and Slovak nationalism will remain an important issue. The Moravians also are demanding greater autonomy. This resurgence of nationalism suggests difficulties for Czechoslovakia in the future, though not necessarily of the same level as in Yugoslavia or the Soviet Union. Nevertheless, these difficulties may blemish the relatively bright spot of the Velvet Revolution. Yet Czechoslovakia has the brightest chances in Eastern Europe.

Hungary has thus far been relatively stable in the transition. Despite this stability, however, Prime Minister Josef Antall and his government face enormous economic problems, including a very substantial foreign debt. They face problems with their neighbor, Romania. While they have some other difficulties because of substantial Hungarian minorities in countries like Yugoslavia and Czechoslovakia, it is the Hungarian minority in Transylvania that has been the most significant issue and has created the biggest problems. Economic difficulties and problems with its neighbors are Hungary's immediate tasks in the future.

In Romania, immense difficulties have arisen in the transition to democracy. These difficulties are understandable after 25 years of tyranny and the revolt that overthrew and executed Nicolae Ceausescu in December 1989. The election of 20 May was marred by some violence and certainly some questions about procedure and process. Ion Iliescu, the president, has been opposed vehemently by people in the urban intelligentsia, particularly in Bucharest and Timisoara. There were riots in June, and Iliescu resorted to calling in miners from a valley north of Bucharest to contain them. The brutality of the miners cast a pallor over the whole electoral process and has set back democratic processes in this country.

In Bulgaria there has been deep trouble with respect to democratic processes. The party headquarters of the former Communists, now the Bulgarian Socialist party, was burned to the ground. This incident just happened a month and a half ago. The Bulgarian Socialists won a narrow electoral victory in June, but whether or not that will have any kind of lasting stability is questionable. Already the new president, who had been part of the opposition, has counseled the population about the possibility of military intervention.

Then there are Yugoslavia and the Soviet Union, the most complex and desperate nations in the Communist world. If Yugoslavia stays as one nation a year from now, I'll be surprised. In Slovenia and Croatia, elections have brought in non–Communist governments. This situation is very different from Serbia, however, where Slobodan Milosevic continues to rule with an iron hand in a Stalinist manner. Milosevic has fermented Serbian nationalism against an Albanian majority in a part of Serbia called Kosovo, where there are deaths almost daily. The Yugoslav future is very cloudy, and the potential of civil war should not be ruled out.

Albania continues to have a Communist ruler. Don't expect that necessarily to last, however. Ramiz Alia had problems just keeping his people in his own country earlier this year as they streamed to foreign embassies to get out.

All of these situations evoke a prognosis that I'm afraid is rather bleak; I wish I could say otherwise. I see some bright spots such as Czechoslovakia and perhaps Hungary. I see some question marks—unrest in the eastern part of Germany and Poland. I see very low prospects for the long-term development of democracy in many parts of the Balkans and even in the Soviet Union.

I don't think that the world can look forward to a quiescent transition. What has been seen in 1989 and 1990 is great news if all one was concerned about was the end of Communist rule; it's less good if one wanted to see a secure development of democracy. It is also troublesome if one is concerned about European security. The massed armies of the Warsaw Pact are no longer present, and there is no longer a Red army that looks completely together; it doesn't have that ominous potential that it once had. The United States has begun to withdraw its own troops from Germany, as has France and Great Britain. The only problem, however, is that earlier in this century unrest in the Balkans lit a larger conflagration.

It was in Sarajevo where the process began that led to 1914. World War II began with the invasion of Poland and not France. There are many things of which people need to be reminded, most notably the volatility of certain parts of Europe. This prognosis is not upbeat. What it does suggest is a heightened responsibility of the United States and other Western democracies to invest in democracy. The West needs to be cognizant that its security now depends on the building and survival of something other than authoritarian systems, and only by investing more, not less, can that security be assured.

QUESTION: I think your appraisal is far too gloomy. Having spent many years living in Eastern Europe, I had an opportunity to make many observations. As for Czechoslovakia, I believe three things are important. First, the people never accepted communism but only lived with it. Second, Czechoslovakia has always been a relatively advanced industrial economy. Third, the ethnic problems that you mentioned are, in my opinion, not that serious.

I think there will be a renaissance in Eastern Europe, but it will take time. Obviously difficulties will be involved in any change this dramatic. The West should be patient and wait.

MR. NELSON: One ought to be patient about Eastern Europe. Patience, however, shouldn't cloud analytical vision. I think the prognosis for Czechoslovakia is much brighter than for some of the other nations. I said that and I do want to reiterate that point. As you pointed out, its economy was better developed, but 45 years of Communist rule has substantially destroyed that economy. The ability of the Czech economy to compete in a world market right now, by their own admission, is rather questionable. Therefore, the period of transition from a planned to an open economy will necessitate the suffering of many people because unprofitable, subsidized enterprises will close and unemployment will rise. Regarding the rise of ethnic nationalism, however, I agree that the Slovak and Moravian minority problems will not be as severe as minority problems in other nations.

QUESTION: You have mentioned several reasons for the demise of the Communist regimes in Eastern Europe. Yet one of the most important reasons is that these regimes were imposed by foreign bayonets and were alien. One shouldn't underestimate the enormous force of suppressed national feeling in all of these countries. It is the dislike of rule from Moscow that has caused a lot of this upheaval, and it is bound for the time being to take a very nationalistic form. Perhaps people should not be too upset by this. The point where I would not agree with you is your regard of nationalism as a negative force. It is a common practice in the American academic world to hold such an opinion.

The other point on which I would like to comment is that I think most of the Eastern Europeans feel that it is the Western Europeans and the European Community above all that ought to be able to help them by extending membership to them. The demand to belong to a wider Europe is strong among the leadership of Eastern Europe. Therefore, it doesn't fall so much to the United States or to Japan; it falls essentially to Western Europe to create the conditions in which these people can gradually be absorbed into a wider Europe, which will help to contain the nationalistic passions and also perhaps provide a certain guarantee of democratic rights and freedoms.

MR. NELSON: I would like to make a comment about whose opinions we are representing. I have heard many Europeans express views dramatically different from yours. In all probability, you are expressing a view that isn't necessarily common to Europe. Neither am I expressing a view that is necessarily common to American academia.

Taking your last point first, the question of who should support these nascent democracies is one about which reasonable people could differ. One ought first to ask who has the resources, however, and then ask who has the responsibility. There are different kinds of resources: monetary and experiential. The United States probably has fewer monetary and far more experiential resources to offer to the democratic transitions in Eastern Europe.

The United States was slow to recognize just how mammoth the changes in Europe were. It should have reacted faster and with more support. It has the so-called SEED I and SEED II Acts (Support of East European Democracy). Yet SEED I provides only $938 million for Poland and Hungary. Prime Minister Kaifu of Japan offered almost $2 billion at about the same time. I think the United States could do more.

QUESTION: What I was saying was that the view that I hear from the Eastern European leaders with whom I have been in touch is that they look to Western Europe. What I mean to address is the way that Eastern Europeans seem to be thinking.

MR. NELSON: Again, I would suggest that it varies considerably as to whom one is talking to and the questions being asked. For example, recently at the Carnegie Endowment a delegation of local administrators from Poland was visiting Washington. These administrators said they could learn absolutely nothing from the Western Europeans, primarily because most of the Western Europeans were engaged in a kind of state-directed economy that they no longer wanted to emulate. Where could they get most of the experience? This was my point about experiential resources.

Supporting these fledgling, post-Communist governments will require the coordinated support of all democratic states. One thing that has been lacking is that kind of overall response from the

European Community (EC) and from the United States cooperating with the EC and Japan. One of the dangers has been the shortfall in that kind of support.

Your point about nationalism is an important one and one that reflects a lot on varying orientations towards the nation-state—what the state is, what nations are, what ethnic identities are, and so on. I believe that nationalism has to be triggered by other antagonisms or concerns. Much of the time nationalism is a sentiment that lies dormant and is largely ineffectual within the political system unless it is triggered by something—for example, the failure of a particular leadership to provide things such as the rule of law, fairness, equity, and economic subsistence.

If those things aren't provided, then nationalism begins to be a very potent force. The question is whether or not it is a good or bad force. Obviously it can be good if it means throwing off the shackles of the Red army. I agree that anti-Soviet or anti-Russian sentiment was very important in Poland and Hungary, given what happened in Hungary in 1956. It was certainly less important, however, in Bulgaria.

Yet how long this nationalistic reaction to a foreign oppressor will continue is dubious. What one sees in Poland now is a reassessment of their relations with the Soviet Union. In fact, the Mazowiecki government initially called for the Soviets to keep their troops longer than planned in East Germany and Poland because Poland's security is at stake.

Therefore, nationalism and its power to be good or bad depends upon being triggered by other needs: economic, political, and security. What I see now is a danger in Eastern Europe that nationalism may move toward being bad—that it may disrupt progress toward democracy, particularly, but not only, in the Balkans. For example, some of the most disruptive forces could be in the right wing in Poland, those demanding that Polish foreign policy seek a return of territories lost to the East after World War II. In Hungary, nationalists in the Democratic Forum or the Smallholders Party could very easily exacerbate tensions with Romania and therefore potentially disrupt democracy. My fear is that nationalism can move in a direction that is damaging to democratic development.

You are correct, therefore, in observing that I don't view nationalism as necessarily a good thing. After World War I, with the linkage of nationalism with statehood, there was reason to see it then as positive. Today, however, I'm not at all convinced, and we should be wary of the power of nationalism to be disruptive to democratic processes.

QUESTION: In your presentation you stated that what happened in Eastern Europe and the Soviet Union in 1989 was not the result of any specific American policy or American foreign policy in general. Instead, you said that the credit lies with the people of those nations. My question is, why did these people do what they did? Is it perhaps because Voice of America broadcasts convinced them that there was a better way of life? Couldn't that have been their motivation?

MR. NELSON: Communications certainly played a role. Like many Americans, I support the Voice of America, Radio Free Europe, and Radio Liberty, as well as the expansion of other kinds of data transfer, like microcomputers, video tapes, and cassette tape recordings. All of these things contributed to a popular or mass recognition in Eastern Europe that there was a better way. I think they knew that anyway, however. I'm one who believes that there is a certain fundamental wisdom in most populations. I have a lot of belief in the masses. One must remember that the first revolts against Communist party rule (particularly in 1953) occurred before Voice of America or Radio Liberty were encouraging people to do so. By 1956 Radio Free Europe was operating and certainly did contribute to the events of 1956 in Hungary. However, these kinds of popular revulsion to authoritarian one-party rule didn't depend on outside information sources. I would be willing to say that Western broadcasts probably accelerated the process somewhat, particularly the distribution of video tapes and cassettes during the 1980s. How that effect can be measured, I don't know.

What Voice of America and others contributed goes back to what I said earlier: popular antipathy because of the failure of the systems. The political systems in Eastern Europe had to be failing for Radio Free Europe, Radio Liberty, the cassettes and the video

70

tapes to have had any effect. If these countries were in fact growing, performing well, and providing goods and services (not just economic but also political services such as the rule of law), perhaps these one-party systems would have worked, and what the world saw last year might not have happened. Simply because they were one-party systems does not mean that revolt was inevitable. It was the failure of these one-party systems to provide for their people that made Voice of America and Radio Free Europe have the impact they did.

QUESTION: Several years ago I read a book by a man named Brian Hall called *Stealing from a Deep Place* in which Hall described his travels through Eastern Europe during the early 1980s. After reading the book, there was absolutely no doubt in my mind that Ceausescu was an absolute tyrant. Yet I can remember the image of Ceausescu in the American press as being a leader in Eastern Europe who dared to oppose the Soviet Union. For this reason he was given enthusiastic receptions on his visits to the West. My question is, didn't they know that this man was a tyrant? If so, why did the United States continue to give him special treatment?

MR. NELSON: I don't know the book, but I agree that the United States certainly made an error of judgment with respect to Ceausescu. It is an error that it has made before and made in many other parts of the world. The United States has often seen relations with a particular dictator as being in its national interest vis-à-vis some larger danger. For many years, of course, that danger was the Soviet Union and world communism. Therefore, because Nicolae Ceausescu sounded like he was anti-Soviet and had a few foreign policies that differed from the Soviet Union, the United States saw him as a maverick and therefore as useful to America.

For years Ceausescu had this image of being anti-Soviet. The United States erroneously assumed that he was anti-Soviet in the same way it was, but he wasn't. Ceausescu was simply intelligent enough to recognize that if he sounded anti-Soviet, he would gain greater credibility in Washington. The United States did correct its image of Ceausescu. The Congress, not the President, began to say there was a problem with the human rights situation in Romania in the mid-1980s, and the United States began to move away from that country. It was too late, though. It should have done it earlier. Unfortunately, the U.S. government regarded Ceausescu as FDR regarded Somoza: He was an S.O.B., but he was our S.O.B. Though he was reprehensible, he was at least on America's side. Nothing could have been further from the truth. He was a bizarre Balkan tyrant, and that picture began to be more and more evident with time.

As I said, Ceausescu was not the only dictator The United States courted. There have been many others. The lesson to learn is that the United States needs to judge leaders not on some vague principle of the national interest vis-à-vis a larger adversary. Instead, it should judge them on the basis of principle, which is stronger, more lasting, and more powerful than any kind of temporary alliance with one of these small dictators.

NARRATOR: Thank you for illuminating the situation in Eastern Europe in the early 1990s.

CHAPTER FIVE

The Presidency Viewed from Eastern Europe: Institutional Change[*]

EUGENE TANTCHEV

NARRATOR: Professor Eugene Tantchev is currently a visiting scholar at the Law School at the University of Virginia. He served for three years as dean of the Law School at the University of Sofia in Bulgaria. He then became a constitutional expert both at the National Round Table and following that in the Grand Assembly Constitutional Committee from 1990 to July 1991. As a result of that body's deliberations, a new constitution for Bulgaria was written and put into effect.

Professor Tantchev is the author of more than 40 publications, including books on presidential power in the United States, First Amendment rights, and the constitutions of liberal democracies. Currently he is engaged in preparing a course on American constitutional law that he will teach at Sofia University.

He is widely regarded as a leading authority on constitutional development in Bulgaria. Inasmuch as on previous occasions other leading scholars have discussed the American presidency from the perspective of their own countries and given the rapid changes throughout the former Communist nations of Eastern Europe, it seems appropriate that Professor Tantchev would discuss that subject today.

---

[*]*Presented in a Forum at the Miller Center of Public Affairs on 9 July 1992.*

MR. TANTCHEV: I will try to give a short outline of the presidency in Central and Eastern European constitutions. I would like to begin with a brief introduction about my country, Bulgaria. Then I will discuss the problem of influences on the democratic transitions, the creation of the institution of the presidency, and finally the various models of heads of state in the West and the presidential institutions of Central and Eastern Europe.

The history of Bulgaria goes back 13 centuries, so it is difficult to describe its history in a short time. The problem is that during those 13 centuries, Bulgaria was under foreign domination for long periods of time. It was under Byzantine domination for two centuries and for another five centuries under the Ottoman Turkish Empire.

Bulgaria was at the crossroads of different civilizations. It had traces of Asian influence, Roman influences, and, of course, Slavic influences. It had proto-Bulgarian influences and many others.

To describe in a short way the history of Bulgaria, I will use one joke that was popular in my country after the transition. The joke is as follows: The Bulgarian president asked President Bush if Bulgaria could join the United States as the next member state. President Bush thought a little while and answered, "Certainly not! Your country was part of the Byzantine Empire, and the Byzantine Empire disappeared. Later, you were in the Ottoman Empire, which also collapsed. You were allies of Germany in two world wars, and Germany lost both wars. You were under Soviet domination, and the Soviet Union and its empire has fallen apart. You are a very dangerous people!"

This joke notwithstanding, Bulgarians are not a dangerous people. The problem is that throughout its history, Bulgaria has not had the luck to be on the right "train." Seemingly always on the wrong train of history, Bulgaria has lost many struggles.

I will focus on the influences in the creation of its constitutions and on the institution of the presidency. There have been several major influences on our constitution making. The first, of course, is Bulgaria's own national traditions. For example, the new democratic constitution is the fourth constitution Bulgaria has had in a little more than 110 years. This fact must be quite amazing to some, because the United States has had only one constitution for over 200 years, but in Europe multiple constitutions are common. If Bulgaria looks for inspiration to France, they have had more than 16 constitutions over the last 200 years.

Another influence on Bulgaria's constitution making stems from models of constitutionalism established in Western democracies. Of course, a very influential source was the American Constitution. Yet another source consists of the international instruments promoting human rights.

Constitutionalism has played and will play a central part in the transition from totalitarianism to democracy. Without constitutionalism, this transition to democracy can be diverted toward an authoritarian path. Still, a big question remains: Can a transition to democracy be made by undemocratic means? Any doctrine or system that has tried to build democracy by undemocratic means was, I would say, a failure. Bulgaria's experience of Communist totalitarianism began with wonderful promises and ideas, as everyone probably knows, but its effort to build democracy undemocratically ended as a complete failure.

Constitutionalism cannot be explained as merely creating a constitution. Many countries with constitutions on paper did not observe constitutional principles, and conversely, some countries with unwritten constitutions embodied strong constitutionalism. Only constitutions that rest on certain fundamental principles and values can be considered a basis for constitutionalism. These fundamental values are the rule of law, separation of powers, respect for human dignity, and human rights.[1]

A central idea for building the presidency was the recognition of the principles of separation of powers and checks and balances. Without those concepts, I don't think a normal presidency can be built. Perhaps that point is obvious for Americans, but it was not obvious for people in my country because Bulgarians have been accustomed to the principle of unity of power. In the context of democratic transitions, it was understood that the legislature should have a supreme role in the machinery of state and in the society. Thus, Bulgaria would only need a nominal president.

It was very difficult to convince the constitution makers in Central and Eastern European countries that a well-constructed presidential institution is of vital importance for democracy. They were reluctant to agree to a president with substantial powers of his own who would serve to limit despotic tendencies in a legislature.

In this area Bulgarians had the example of American constitutionalism. I could not help but cite a piece from Alexander Hamilton, who stated in *The Federalist* No. 70 why a democratic system is in need of a very strong president with limited powers.

> Energy in the executive is a leading character in the definition of good government. . . . A feeble executive implies a feeble execution of the government. A feeble execution is but another phrase for a bad execution; and a government ill executed, whatever it may be in theory, must be, in practice, a bad government.[2]

This thought influenced Bulgaria's constitution making with regard to the need for a well-constructed presidency.

Perhaps the easiest way to characterize Central and Eastern European presidents would be to say that they are somewhere in the scale between the French model of the presidency and the German or Italian model.[3] This categorization is partly true but is also quite inaccurate. In order to characterize the presidents in Central and Eastern European countries, I will give a brief overview of the institutional models of heads of state in history and contemporary times.

The institution of the head of state is a necessary prerequisite in every constitutional scheme. The only exception so far known is the Jacobin Constitution in France of 1793, which lasted less than two years. Its example was not followed, as far as I know, in any other country. There are many reasons why this is true, but I will not dwell on that subject.

A confederacy does not establish the institution of head of state. This form simply reflects that these are alliances of fully sovereign states, each of which have their own heads of state. It was so in the Articles of Confederation in the United States. It is so, for example, in the Swiss confederation. Their "head of state" is an executive council composed of seven members, who change their positions on the principle of rotation.

In addition to being used in the Swiss confederation, the collective head-of-state model was established under the Stalinist constitutions, and so-called presidiums or state councils were created. In fact, they proved to be a contradiction in objective because they were theoretically intended to limit the power of a single despot, but in fact they served the opposite goal. Rather than limiting the power of the party general secretary who presided over them, they merely rubber-stamped his decisions. Yugoslavia also used to have a very interesting kind of collective head of state, but owing to the civil war, that belongs to the past. It would be quite inappropriate for me to classify, as Aristotle and his followers did, the models of the heads of state according to whether they were hereditary or elective, because there are so many differences within these two groups.[4]

Among singular heads of state, there are at least four models of monarchies. Absolute monarchy does not belong to the past as most people think because about six states in the world still have that form, including the Vatican, which is a special case, as well as some Arab states. The very rare form of elective monarchy prevailed for several centuries in Poland but now exists in only one state of the Third World. There is also dualistic monarchy, and that form which is most common in Western Europe, the parliamentary constitutional monarchy.

Among republican heads of states, there is the institution of presidency, of which there are at least four models. The American presidency created here was a lasting and profound institution that had never before existed in the world.

Western Europe and now Central and Eastern Europe as well have parliamentary presidents. These presidents are merely nominal heads of states. The office of president in the French Fifth Republic is a very interesting, special model. It is the parliamentary-presidential, or sometimes the presidential-parliamentary, model of government, depending on the parliamentary majorities that form the cabinet and party and the party affiliation of the president.[5] The last model of the presidency is that which is now emerging in some Islamic countries. This model was put into practice for the first time by the Islamic Constitution of Iran but happily has not influenced Eastern European countries. It is very difficult to define it within the normal constitutional framework because the Iranian president serves under the supervision of the spiritual leader of the country.[6]

In Central and Eastern Europe, one can see presidencies of three kinds, but all of them are situated somewhere along the scale I mentioned—between a parliamentary model typified by Italy and Germany and the parliamentary-presidential model, which is given by the Fifth Republic of France. The Romanian office of president is very similar to that of the French Fifth Republic; in Article 80 of the Romanian Constitution, the formula of the French Constitution is nearly repeated. One can also see this model in the Polish Constitution and in the Croat Constitution. The German parliamentary model was emulated by the Hungarian Constitution, and the Hungarian head of state is a nominal president. Somewhere between the two poles of that scale the Bulgarian and Czechoslovak presidents can be found.

It was difficult to agree on the mode of electing the presidents in Bulgaria, and much controversy had to be overcome. There are two modes of electing presidents in Central and Eastern Europe. The directly elected president shows the influence of the French model. Presidents are directly elected in Romania, Bulgaria, Poland, Russia, and some of the other republics of the former Soviet Union.

Presidents are elected by the Parliament in Hungary and in the Czechoslovak Constitution. Speaking about Czechoslovakia, there is the big question of its separation. From the standpoint of the presidency, it is very interesting that President Havel was not reelected and resigned. It will be quite interesting from the standpoint of constitutionalism how this Czechoslovak state will manage to exist without a president until its separation.

Debate on the election of the president was a crucial point in the drafting of the constitution. The constituent assembly in Bulgaria spent a lot of its time on this part. Likewise, in the drafting of the American Constitution, the mode of electing the president was one of the most difficult questions that the Founding Fathers had to resolve.

The experience of the Founding Fathers helped Bulgarians to decide on that question. In the final debates, there were very sound

78

arguments against parliamentary or congressional election of the president. It was said that such a system would infringe on separation of powers; it would not provide for checks and balances; it would not constrain the will of the majority of the assembly; and that it could thus evolve, as Thomas Jefferson had said earlier, into legislative despotism.

Another argument was that parliamentary election of the president would lead to a lot of intrigues and fighting among factions in the assembly. That point was, in fact, proved 200 years later by the Czechoslovak experience and the first democratic presidential election in Bulgaria. Bulgaria's current president was elected for his first term by parliament before the drafting of the constitution. The experience of its constituent assembly demonstrated how thoughtful the American Founding Fathers were.[7]

Bulgarians prepared 21 different drafts before the constituent assembly started to work on the constitution. One of them proposed reestablishing the monarchy in Bulgaria. A draft prepared by Professor Bernard Siegan from the University of San Diego Law School was shaped under the influence of the American presidency. About seven drafts called for parliamentary election of the president. All of the other drafts contained provisions for the direct election of the president.

Obviously, the mode of the election of presidents is related to their powers and their position in the whole constitutional scheme. This is a rule, but in Europe there are several exceptions to that rule. Austria and Finland have directly elected presidents with quite limited powers who function in the framework of parliamentary states. Bulgaria tried this method but was only partly successful, unfortunately. In the constitutional assembly, some of the powers of the presidency in the original drafts were circumscribed.

I will try briefly to systematize the powers of Central and Eastern European presidents. The first group of presidential powers are those regarding legislation. Presidents do not have the right to initiate legislation, but the Bulgarian president may initiate constitutional amendments. Bulgarian presidents have only a limited kind of veto power, which is seen in the French Fifth

Republic's Constitution. It is the power to force the reconsideration of laws. If a president does not sign the law and returns it to the assembly, the assembly is obliged to reconsider the law. The law can then only be passed with an absolute majority. The absolute majority requirement is a safeguard compared to the simple majority, but not as much of one as the two-thirds majority veto override requirement.

Some of the presidents, especially the Romanian and Polish ones, have the power to call for referendums. This is a very strong power that can be used against the parliament as a direct appeal to the people. The Romanian and Bulgarian presidents can also directly address the assembly as well as the nation.

In the executive sphere, there are differences depending on which model of president is used. If it is the French model, as in Poland and Romania, executive power is divided between the government and prime minister on one side and the president on the other. In a parliamentary system, the president is outside of the realm of the executive power. He is essentially a nominal head of state.

Presidents designate and invest prime ministers to form governments in Central and Eastern European countries, but these prime ministerial candidates can only be appointed if they receive a vote of confidence in the assembly. Some presidents can dissolve parliament if they are unable to form a government, contrary to American practice. They also have the power to issue orders and regulations. Some of the stronger presidents who are closer to the American and French models are commanders-in-chief of the armed forces. That is true of the Bulgarian, Romanian, and Polish presidents. The Hungarian president is not commander-in-chief, however.

Presidents are entitled to declare martial law but are obliged to obtain the approval of parliament. Interestingly, under the Bulgarian Constitution, the Intelligence Office is directly subordinated to the president. Under the normal parliamentary model, these institutions are connected to the government and particularly with the ministry of interior. Parliamentary oversight on the intelligence is crucially important in the democratic states.

In the sphere of foreign relations, presidents have a leading role in negotiating treaties. They receive and appoint ambassadors, and they have the power to recognize foreign governments.

Although judicial power properly belongs to the independent courts, presidents do have the right to pardon convicts or to correct injustices that a court may have committed. They also have the power to appoint some of the justices of constitutional courts and some of the supreme justices. The others are appointed by the assembly.

Central and Eastern European presidents are not held responsible on political grounds, in fact, but a system of presidential responsibility is being established in the new democratic constitutions. Here again, the American experience was very useful. The only grounds on which Eastern and Central European presidents can be impeached are breach of oath and breach of the constitution.

In the impeachment process, the investigation is to be conducted by the Bulgarian parliament, but the trial is to be conducted by the constitutional courts. This division of functions is very important, because in most Central and Eastern European countries the assemblies are not bicameral, as in the United States and some countries in Western Europe, but unicameral. If all of these stages of impeachment were to be conducted in the assembly alone, the presidency would be very dangerous and unstable, as history has proven, for it would depend on the legislature's good will.

I will conclude my short overview with an observation on the impact that personality has on the institution of president. A very important role is being played by the character of the individuals who are the presidents in Central and Eastern European countries now. There is something very peculiar with the revolution and related events all taking place. Only a few people can stand alone upon the web of popularity. Sometimes the most popular and outstanding dissidents in Central and Eastern European countries were elected president. But as history and events taking place in these countries prove, it is very difficult for them to remain on this web of popularity. When the institutional power is exercised by a very popular man, the office is much stronger than when they are exercised by a man whose popularity is fading.

I will end with a good thought from Alexis de Tocqueville, who noted that the powers of the presidency not only derive from having been drafted in the constitution. His conclusion was later reconfirmed by such scholars as Edwin Corwin, Louis Koenig, and Clinton Rossiter: Powers delegated by a constitution can make a president very strong, but the real conditions of political life can circumscribe his possible actions.[8]

QUESTION: You didn't touch on how long the term of the president should be and whether an incumbent should be eligible for reelection.

MR. TANTCHEV: That is a very important question and was controversial in some countries. However, in my country it was generally accepted that the president could serve only two consecutive terms. That model was established not only in the Bulgarian Constitution but also in the Romanian, Polish, and Hungarian constitutions. I am not sure about Czechoslovakia because they did not succeed in adopting a wholly new democratic constitution, but have only amended their old constitution. These two consecutive terms are either four or five years each in the various countries.

I am not sure how this problem could be resolved by a succession in terms by a vice president because no one has yet had that experience in Central and Eastern European countries. In Bulgaria the vice president is entitled to inherit the presidency if some unfortunate event takes place or if the president is removed. Limited terms of office and the principle of rotation are very important safeguards against a new authoritarian or even totalitarian regime in emerging democracies.

It is very difficult to make this transition in a democratic way because old stereotypes are still alive. Authoritarian or communist thinking is in evidence not only among the old Communist parties (now called "Socialist") but among the common people who lack democratic traditions. So this principle for conscribing presidential terms of office is very important.

QUESTION: In the wake of the revolutions, we have seen Havel and Walesa lose their once firm grasp on authority. Given the history of foreign domination, as well as the cultural and ethnic situation that prevails in that part of the world, what do you expect will happen with constitutional democracy?

MR. TANTCHEV: As everyone knows, things are not going so smoothly. At first there was great enthusiasm, and it was thought that the transition would be very fast. People assumed it would be enough just to create the constitutional framework of democratic institutions and conduct some economic reforms, and everything would be settled. I am not a specialist in the sphere of economics, but it is probably the most difficult obstacle to successful transition. Even for Germany, the process of reintegration will take place over five or even ten years, with huge sums of money invested in the eastern regions that had been separated for 50 years.

Nationalistic ideas have filled the vacuum that was left by the defunct Communist ideology. The most drastic examples are seen in Yugoslavia and some republics of the former Soviet Union. It is very difficult to predict how things will go, especially in light of recent developments in Yugoslavia.

Speaking about my country, most ethnic problems have been resolved, but they could be rekindled very fast. All of the Balkan wars and most wars in Eastern Europe have started from and about Macedonia, which is now in a very difficult situation. It has not gained as much foreign recognition as have the other former Yugoslav republics. It is recognized by Bulgaria, however. In some periods of history, Macedonia was a part of Bulgaria. It is not recognized by its other neighbor, Greece, which claims Macedonia to be part of Greece. If the Yugoslav federal army moves against Macedonia, I don't know what will happen in my country and in Greece, Turkey, or elsewhere.

QUESTION: In the United States, normally two candidates run for president. This year, the country has the dubious privilege of having three, which tends to confuse the voters. A number of countries in Europe have multiple political parties, as many as 25. That large number of parties tends to make a weakened government with a coalition. How many parties does Bulgaria have and how do the elections proceed?

MR. TANTCHEV: After the fall of a totalitarian regime that was characterized by a one-party system merged with the state machinery, a large number of parties always appears. Bulgaria didn't set a world record for this number. It had approximately 100 parties, some of which were ridiculous with just a handful of followers. As far as I know, the record belongs to Portugal, which had about 270 parties in the first elections after the fall of Salazar's regime in 1974. Twenty-six candidates had registered for the presidential elections, but only three of them had any serious chances.

America always has many minor candidates for the presidency. Even here in Charlottesville, I saw people signing a petition for president. Of course, only the two major parties have a real chance of winning the election. I don't know if that situation is good for American democracy; it is a question that Americans can understand better for themselves. There was an American author who wrote that there are a lot of tombstones representing the failed ambitions of third parties in America.

In these transitions, a two-, three-, or even a four-party system is just not feasible. A party system is always reemerging and forming. Bulgaria didn't have a normal civil society or normal social strata under Communist rule. Thus, it will take a long time before Bulgaria has some kind of settled party system.

It has a proportional representation in parliament, but a party must win a threshold of 4 percent of the vote in the country in order to get a seat in parliament. That system didn't serve well in Bulgaria in the last elections because now only three parties represented are in Parliament. Outside the parliament there are many parties that could be considered serious, with a substantial number of followers.

In Poland, unlimited proportional representation has not served well, as one can see. It produced a parliament composed of 16 or 17 parties, some of them having won barely 1 percent of the vote. Things are quite unstable now in Poland as a result.

QUESTION: I have two questions related to the Islamic community in Bulgaria. First, are the majority of Moslems there Shi'ite or Sunni? Second, you mentioned that the Islamic Constitution was formulated on the Iranian model. You also mentioned other types of constitutions. As people know and have seen from the experience of the last ten years, Islamic political movements tend to clash with Western ideology, thinking, and way of life. Bulgaria, by its proximity and history, falls pretty much within Western thinking and the Western way of life. Has the Islamic community in Bulgaria made any attempt to form a constitution that would be more compatible and harmonious with the Western way of thinking?

MR. TANTCHEV: First, I would like to say that of course the Iranian Constitution is much more unique than the general model it holds out to the whole Islamic world. As everyone knows, there are different currents in the Islamic religion.

The Iranian model is a model for a fundamentalist Islamic constitution. For example, Turkey is a mostly Islamic country, but the Turkish Constitution is certainly not based on the Iranian model. It is much closer to the Western European model of the presidency.

To the best of my knowledge the Islamic community in Bulgaria did not put forth ideas to have an Islamic constitution. No such draft was introduced in the constituent assembly. The Islamic community comprises about one-tenth of the population of Bulgaria, but they have much more political influence than that. In Bulgaria's Parliament only three parties are represented after the elections of October 1991: the ruling coalition of parties known as the Union of Democratic Forces (UDF); the Bulgarian Socialist party; and the Movement for Rights and Freedoms in Bulgaria, most of whose members have an Islamic outlook. In effect, according to liberal democratic political theory, Bulgaria has a two-and-a-half party system because this Turkish party holds the balance of power in parliament and thus can decide major questions. This small "half" party can decide which of the parties can form the government and takes advantage of its position.

NARRATOR: Before the discussion you and I were talking about the fact that the Socialist party, in effect, is the former Communist party. But even beyond that, most of the active political people were in one way or another former Communists. A colleague who isn't here today asked a very interesting question of the visitors from the Soviet Union. He asked, "Is there any effort to present in a more widespread way the ideas of democracy and democratic governance, given the fact that until very recently people were committed to another kind of politics and governance?"

MR. TANTCHEV: That is a big question. As I mentioned, it is not only a matter of building democratic institutions because they can be used as a mere rubber stamp. Having been brought up and educated in this undemocratic tradition, many people have simply chosen one or the other party with no solid basis for judgment. But with difficulty, they are changing their outlook and are gradually coming to understand the democratic process.

It is true that the members of the Bulgarian Socialist party, most of the socialist parties in Central and Eastern Europe, the Romanian movement of President Iliescu, and even most followers of the current Russian president are former Communists. In the now ruling democratic parties there are certainly many former Communists, and it is simply not possible to understand the nature of the Communist party. One cannot compare it with an American party. American parties, as described by Moisei Ostrogorski and James Bryce until nowadays don't have formal party membership.[9] Nor do they have such big machinery as the parties in Eastern and Central Europe and especially the Communist parties during the totalitarian era. While the membership of the French Socialist party did not exceed 250,000, Communist party membership was counted in millions in each country—the largest being the Communist party of the Soviet Union (CPSU) with more than 15 million. The Bulgarian Communist party had more than one million members.

Many people have changed their party affiliation, but it is more difficult to change their understanding of how democracy works. It is very difficult to describe European liberals and compare them to American liberals. Democratic liberals in

86

America may be much closer ideologically to social democracy in Western Europe.

It is very difficult, also, to compare conservatives in Central and Eastern Europe, and especially nationalist conservatives, with American conservatives. There is no direct correlation.

NARRATOR: We are very grateful for this clear and coherent presentation on the governments of your own country and of Eastern and Central Europe in general. We hope you will come back and talk more about the transition to democratic constitutionalism, and particularly about some of the issues that you touched on toward the end.

ENDNOTES

1. Ch. H. McIlwain, *Constitutionalism: Ancient and Modern*, New York, 1947, 21-22. A.E.D. Howard, "The Road to Constitutionalism," Virginia Commission on Bicentennial of the U.S. Constitution, 1990. H. van Marseveen, G. v. der Tang, *Written Constitutions*, New York, 1978. G. Sartori, "Constitutionalism," *American Political Science Review*, v. 56, 1962, 853.

2. Al. Hamilton, J. Madison, J. Jay, *The Federalist*, ed. Fletcher Wright, Cambridge, No. 70, 451.

3. For a different approach and treatment of the Bulgarian and Romanian Constitutions and presidencies, compare S. Holmes, J. Elster, "New Constitutions Adopted in Bulgaria and Romania," *Eastern European Constitutional Review*, v. I, N. 1, Spring 1992, 11-12.

4. Aristotle, *Politics*, Book III, Ch. 5. St. Thomas Aquinas, *On Kingship*, Toronto, 1949. Marsilio of Padua, *The Defender of Peace*, Columbia University Press, 1952.

5. Guy Carcassome, France (1958): *The Fifth Republic After Thirty Years in Constitutions in Democratic Politics*, ed. V. Bogdanoz, Aldershot, 1988, 241. W. Safran, *The French Polity*, Longman, 1991, 130. M. Duverger, *The Study of Politics*, Nelson, 1979, 82.

6. Constitution of the Islamic Republic of Iran in art. 60 provides that "The Executive power shall be vested in the President and the Ministers except in those cases in which according to the Constitution, it is vested in a Leader." According to art. 110 the leader is commander in chief, and he confirms the appointment of the president after his election by the people. What is probably most interesting and unique is paragraph 10 of art. 110, the Spiritual Leader is entitled to . . . dismiss the President " . . . in the interests of the country after a judgment of the Supreme Court, regarding violations of presidential duties or by the verdict of the Islamic Consultative Assembly declaring the President incompetent." A. P. Blaunstein, G. H. Flanz, *Constitutions of the Countries of the World*, vol. VI, May 1992.

7. *Records of the Federal Convention of 1787*, ed. M. Farrand, Chicago, 1966, v. II, 103-104.

8. "The Laws allow him to be strong, but circumstances keep him weak." A. de Tocqueville, *Democracy in America*, 1945, v. I, 126. E. Corwin, *The President: Office and Powers*, New York, 1984, 26-28. L. Koenig, *The Chief Executive*, New York, 1986, 96-98. Cl. Rossiter, *American Presidency*, New York, 1962, 46-61.

9. M. Ostrogorski, *Democracy and Organization of Political Parties*, New York, 1970, v. II.

III.

COUNTRY PROBLEMS
AND PERSPECTIVES

Constitutional and Political Developments in Hungary*

PETER PACZOLAY

MR. PACZOLAY: I am happy to be at the University of Virginia and the Miller Center, and I thank you for the opportunity to speak on constitutional and political developments in Hungary and Eastern and Central Europe.

The drafting of Hungary's new constitution was begun by the Communist government in 1988 and 1989. The so-called reformist wing of the Communist government decided to move the Hungarian political system closer to the rule of law and Western standards of democracy. While political forces were working on a new constitution in the summer of 1989, it was very hot, as it was 200 years ago when America was drafting its constitution in Philadelphia. (Maybe hot summers are good for writing constitutions.) During that summer, the governing Communist party and the opposition (which at that time included all opposition forces, some of whom have since joined the new Hungarian government) sat down to discuss constitutional issues. Both sides agreed that instead of drafting a new constitution, they would revise the existing one, which was written in 1949. Their intention was to introduce new principles into the constitution, including a bill of rights. Both sides also agreed to leave the drafting of a new

---

Presented in a Forum at the Miller Center of Public Affairs on 22 January 1991. Peter Paczolay is a graduate of Eötvös Loránd University in Budapest and is on the faculty of that university. He is the chief counselor at Hungary's Constitutional Court.

constitution to a freely elected parliament, and not to the Parliament that was elected in 1985, of which 75 percent of the representatives were members of the Communist party.

This revised constitution was promulgated on 23 October 1989—the anniversary of the 1956 Hungarian Revolution. Some of the revisions included the separation of powers, the rule of law, a multiparty political system, and a market economy. These are the basic principles on which this revised constitution was based, a constitution that was designed to serve during the period of transition from socialism to democracy and to a market system. At the same time that this constitution was promulgated, a number of new institutions were established, including the Constitutional Court.

This constitution was again amended after the free elections. The core of the new amendments served to cancel those provisions from the first revision that were the results of the compromise between the Communist party and the opposition. For example, in the first revision references remained to the value of socialism. The second revised constitution has eliminated all such references to socialism and its so-called value. Instead, it guarantees the right to private property, which was not very strongly emphasized in the first basic revision of the constitution, and other basic rights as well.

So the governmental system in Hungary now is a parliamentary democracy, based on the supremacy of Parliament. The Parliament is balanced, however, by the executive power of the president, the judicial power of the courts, and the Constitutional Court, which is independent from the ordinary judiciary branch. Under this new system, the Parliament has the right to amend the constitution and decide on questions of war and peace. The leader of the majority in the Parliament is the prime minister in Hungary, which means that the executive branch depends upon the decisions of this faction in Parliament. The executive depends upon his parliamentary majority as in the English cabinet system, but not to as great an extent.

Presently, the majority faction in the Parliament is a coalition composed of three political parties having a 59 percent majority of the seats. The largest is the Hungarian Democratic Forum (which is also the largest party in the nation), followed by the Smallholders party and the Christian Democratic party. The present government is usually considered to be relatively conservative, believing in more traditional Hungarian values such as national feeling and the role of religion.

What is most interesting is that the Free Democrats, an opposition party, are more anticommunist than the so-called right-wing parties that comprise the governing coalition. Another opposition party, the Young Democrats, was formed three years ago as an alternative to the Young Communists organization, which was traditionally the only organization for young people in Hungary as well as in all other socialist countries. The Young Democrats organization was formed mostly of students from the law school. Thirty of them formed this organization, which later became a political party but which initially was simply a youth organization. Presently, all of its members are under 35 years of age. Of course, in two or three years, they will modify the age requirement. It is basically a liberal party, mostly following American liberal values. In fact, many of these students later came to the United States to do their postgraduate studies and were influenced by American liberal thought while they were here. They are now a political force as well, and in the local government election they were the third major party in Hungary. The Young Democrats not only attract the support of younger voters, they also attract support from the oldest voting group in the country. A final note on the Young Democrats is that they are in the *Guinness Book of World Records* as having the youngest elected members of any national parliament in the world—their average age being in the 20s.

The sixth party represented in the Parliament is the former Communist party, which has transformed itself into a social democratic party. This party has divided the opposition because the other two opposition groups (the Free Democrats and the Young Democrats) don't want to vote with a socialist party. Therefore, there is opposition even within the opposition, as everyone is against this new social democratic party. This will be going on for about two or three years at least.

Hungary now has a president of the republic, an office without much history in that country. Only from 1946 until 1949 did Hungary have a president, so it is unusual in Hungarian history to have one at all. Now it is returning to that system, and the president has almost the same powers he did after World War II. The president's main task is to represent the country as its head of state. He can, in very specific and rare cases, dissolve the Parliament. He is the commander in chief of the army, although it is controlled by a parliamentary commission, even in times of war. Also, the president appoints all judges.

In regard to the judiciary branch, Hungary has many judges whose views survived the 40 years of communism and are based not on political values but on legal values. While it was common in the 1950s and even after the Hungarian Revolution in 1956 to have trials whose outcomes were decided by the Communist party (as in the Soviet Union), by about 1965 political trials in Hungary had become less and less frequent. The reason for this difference is that the opposition in Hungary was very weak. Only a few intellectuals really protested, and so the government, at least in the last 10 to 15 years, tolerated opposition. Unlike Havel in Czechoslovakia or Walesa in Poland, Hungary did not have these kinds of political heros.

Hungary has guarantees for the independence of its judiciary, which means, for example, that they cannot be members of any political party. This provision actually dates from 1988 when the Communists were still in power. The judges had to leave the Communist party and were not allowed to be members of any other political party. All of the judges are appointed by the president of the republic. This provision means that they choose to become judges as a career, and they do so at a very early age. Therefore, they become oriented towards legal and not political thought because of their curriculum. After graduating, they serve as law clerks in the courts for two years. They have to take a special exam, and after that exam they become a magistrate similar to magistrates in the American federal judicial system. At this point they are not yet deciding cases—although occasionally they are allowed to make decisions in minor cases—but instead are performing various tasks in the legal system. For example, before a divorce trial they conduct briefings with each party, perhaps trying to persuade them not to go through with the divorce.

I should add that even though the president appoints all judges where there is a vacancy, sometimes it is the minister of justice or a special judicial conference that actually appoints a nominee. In these instances, the president simply signs the official nomination papers.

The Hungarian judicial system has three levels. First, there are the local courts that have general jurisdiction. Second, there are the 20 county courts. Third, there is the Supreme Court. All three levels have jurisdiction over almost all areas, but they do not decide on constitutional issues. This area is the job of the independent Constitutional Court.

The idea of judiciary review is quite new in Europe. It was introduced by Hans Kelsen in 1920 to the Austrian legal system as an independent constitutional court. The idea didn't really work, however, and it wasn't until after World War II that the idea of judicial review became popular. Germany, Italy, Spain, Portugal, and now even Yugoslavia and Poland have adopted this principle through the establishment of independent constitutional courts.

Why do they have independent constitutional courts? Over the years, the judiciaries in all of these countries have been afraid of ruling on constitutional issues. In fact, they have expressly rejected doing this task. In many of the nations of Europe, judges were trained to have a positivist attitude toward the law whereby parliaments created laws that could not be reviewed. Many believe that this attitude toward the law was one of the causes of the Nazi regime in Germany. All laws were accepted as rigid and never questioned. Therefore, the *Grundgesetz*, or Basic Law of West Germany, with the help of American constitutional lawyers, developed the independent German Constitutional Court to decide on all issues raised in other courts or by any German citizen.

The Hungarian Constitutional Court has a very broad jurisdiction, even compared to other similar courts in Europe. It reviews bills before enactment. It reviews all statutes and even other legal norms, by which I mean sublegislative norms—regulations that were not enacted by the Parliament but instead were issued by the executive branch. Because of the socialist legal heritage, Hungary has many of these sublegislative norms. The court also has jurisdiction over conflicts concerning competencies between state

95

organs and local governments and between different local governments. Finally, the court has jurisdiction over the impeachment of the president of the republic. All other high officials are under the jurisdiction of the Parliament.

What differentiates the Hungarian Constitutional Court from the American Supreme Court is that Hungary's court not only interprets the constitution through actual cases (as does the U.S. Supreme Court), but it also advises and interprets the constitution on abstract questions. When the Constitutional Court rules on the constitutionality of a legal statute, its decision is binding on the Hungarian Supreme Court. Its decisions are also binding on all other lower courts, administrative agencies, the executive, and the Parliament. Only the Parliament has the power to review the decisions of the Constitutional Court—through the former's power to amend the constitution. However, this has not happened during the first year.

The judges of the Constitutional Court are elected by the Parliament. There are ten judges at this moment, and all of them were elected by the Parliament for nine years. All other judges, however, are appointed for life tenure in Hungary. This provision is basically new because under the Communists, judges were elected by the local governments. That means they were nominated by the Communist party. Therefore, in Hungary, the idea of the election and the recall of judges by public opinion is rejected. Only the judges of the Constitutional Court are elected.

One of the differences between what Hungary is doing on constitutional matters and what is happening in other Eastern European countries is that in the other countries there is a greater effort to write their constitutions quickly. Poland, Czechoslovakia, Romania, and Bulgaria are all now working very hard on new constitutions that they hope to promulgate within the next year. Hungary is going to wait two or three years. Many people in government, academia, and the private sector are working on constitutional issues; however, Hungary is going to wait and see how the new institutions are working before it promulgates a new one. Basically, the Hungarian constitution that will be promulgated within a few years will not be a completely new constitution introducing new institutions to the Hungarian political and legal system. It will legitimize the present governmental and political system while making many practical corrections. Therefore, there will be some basic changes in this system, and so this new constitution will probably be the subject of a popular referendum.

The other countries are now looking for new institutions and new systems of government. Czechoslovakia is having difficulty trying to develop federal systems. They cannot find a way out of this trap of how to build a federal system between two countries, given that all government agencies were in Prague. They don't know how to move some of them to Slovakia, and the Czechs are completely rejecting the idea of sharing power. Romania is also in a very difficult situation. It is not clear if there was really a democratic change in the political system or if it was only a coup d'etat by some forces within the former ruling class. These countries, then, have very short project times for developing new constitutions. Hungarians consider themselves to be in a better situation.

QUESTION: You said that during the mid-1980s judges in Hungary did not face the same political pressures from the ruling Communist party as their colleagues in other Eastern European nations did. Why didn't they? What is it about Hungary and its political system that kept it further removed from the political pressures?

MR. PACZOLAY: Even today Hungarians do not know how the real decisions were made during the former regime of János Kádár. These decisions were made in a very close circle of people, and I think that Kádár himself made most of the decisions because he was very suspicious of all of the other central committee members. Though it is not clear why, he decided to pursue a more democratic path compared to the other countries of Eastern Europe at that time.

One of the decisions Kádár made was to allow the judiciary to rule on cases based upon their own values and not upon political pressure from the party. Even today, of course, Hungary's criminal law system doesn't fully protect the rights of the defendants. It is not even considered to be democratic, even though the criminal justice system is now being reformed, including the prison system.

Therefore, Hungary is in the modeling stage of shaping new guarantees and a new criminal procedure.

The civil law that has been in place since the Hungarian Civil Code was enacted in 1959 has worked quite well. Only the regulations in it regarding property have to be changed. The right to private property is the opposite of the former socialist position of the Hungarian legal system. Everything used to be owned by the society or by the state. Speaking in more sociological terms, it was owned by the very small ruling class who owned all of the wealth in the country. This part of the Civil Code will of course have to be changed.

QUESTION: In layman's language, could you say that the Constitutional Court is a "super Supreme Court"? You said that it was above the Supreme Court. Does that mean that in effect it really is a super Supreme Court that handles fewer cases and is looked on in a different way? Is it perhaps a specialized court?

MR. PACZOLAY: It is specialized in that it deals only with constitutional issues, for example, when during a trial a constitutional issue is raised. Of course, ordinary judges could rule on these questions; however, unless they are very ambitious, most do not. Therefore, they send the file to the Constitutional Court, which decides, for example, whether the statute on which a lower judge once based his decision is constitutional or not. When this decision is made, the court sends the case back to the lower court, which then rules in the concrete case.

Also, the court's decisions are binding upon the Supreme Court. It does not revise Supreme Court decisions, however, nor is it a court of appeals. This means that when a decision is handed down in a lower court, it may only be challenged on the grounds that the statute on which the final decision was based is unconstitutional. This challenge is called a constitutional complaint. It is more or less modeled on the German system, *Verfassungsbeschwerde*, in which the decisions of all government agencies may be challenged on constitutional grounds.

QUESTION: What role does legal precedent play in the Hungarian judicial system?

MR. PACZOLAY: The Hungarian legal system tradition is based on Roman law and is influenced historically by the Austrian and consequently by the German legal systems. For example, before the Second World War, Hungarian civil law was based on precedent because Hungary did not have a civil code until 1959. Thus, until 1959 the Supreme Court decisions were basically the sources of law in civil cases. Hungary didn't have a civil code, so civil laws were based on precedent. Therefore, the idea of precedence is not so alien for Hungarians as perhaps it is for those in the other countries of the area.

QUESTION: During the Communist era, from the mid-1940s to about 1989, Czechoslovakia was a much more Stalinist and rigidly controlled country. In Prague recently I had dinner with the vice dean of the law faculty at Charles University, who said that out of 127 members of the law faculty at that university, exactly six had not been members of the Communist party. How those six slipped through is unclear. The other 121 may not have all been true believers, but they did at least join for career purposes. This fact was true for all academic disciplines (especially the social sciences and professions), although to a lesser extent in the pure sciences of chemistry or physics, for example.

It certainly would be true in Czechoslovakia that one would have some difficulty assuming that a judge who had served under the ancient regime could suddenly accept the premises of the new order of democracy and change his thought patterns. It seems, therefore, that there are two things that a judiciary in Hungary has to confront and surmount to be truly effective in protecting the constitution. One, as mentioned, is to move away from the traditional European deference to Parliament. The notion of parliamentary supremacy dies hard in Europe, and it is very difficult for a judge to confront Parliament and say that it has violated the constitution. The second is the legacy of the Communist era. How serious do you think these two issues are in Hungary, and how serious do you think they will be in standing in the way of a new generation of judges who would be in fact part of the democratic principle?

MR. PACZOLAY: That is a difficult question. What you mentioned concerning Communist party memberships in Czechoslovakia for professors was true for Hungary as well during the 1960s and the early 1970s. Because of my age, however, I am luckier because I wasn't even tempted to become a member of the Communist party. It was no longer a requirement for a member of the faculty to be a member of the Communist party in the 1980s. The Communist party went through some very big crises in these last years, so actually all of the faculty members in the law schools left the Communist party. Of course, the judges were forced to leave the party, and they did it, I think, willingly and without objection.

An important issue now in Hungary is how to treat those people who were members of the Communist party. Should they be prosecuted, or should Hungarians be permissive and adopt a Christian attitude toward them? It would be best to get rid of some of those people who were very involved in the party, perhaps remove them from whatever office they hold without actually prosecuting them. After all, it is not feasible to deprive 800,000 people of their rights because they were members of the Communist party, especially since many of them had joined the party for the sake of their career or simply to survive.

Your point about changing the way in which judges who served under the Communist regime think is well-taken, and this is now a big problem for the Hungarian judiciary. It will probably take about ten years to train a new, younger generation of judges who will have different attitudes toward and different interpretations of the law and will not always have to rely on the interpretations of the Supreme Court.

In Hungary's system, the Supreme Court enforces its decisions on the other courts in order to make the decisions and jurisdictions of these courts more uniform. They can also reverse the decisions of lower courts if they believe these have contradicted any of the Supreme Court's previous decisions. As I said, it will probably take a decade before Hungary will have judges who will not rely solely on the decisions of this court.

QUESTION: Could you provide some examples of recent rulings by the Constitutional Court? Has the court declared any legislative acts unconstitutional, and if so, have any of these been of major significance? Also, how well has the principle of limited government—which is essential to guarantee individual liberties—taken hold in Hungary? Has the Parliament in any way been able to limit the powers of the Constitutional Court?

MR. PACZOLAY: In its first year, the Constitutional Court heard 600 cases. One of the main subjects of the court's decisions has been the concept of equal protection and equal rights before the law. This concept arose most often in cases of sex discrimination in areas such as labor law, social security regulations, and social welfare regulations. The Constitutional Court declared unconstitutional several provisions of Hungary's social welfare system because they discriminated against men: for example, regulations which allowed pensions for women who were widowed but not for men who were widowed. In labor law, the situation was reversed. Many statutes discriminated against women, and these statutes were declared unconstitutional by the court.

A second subject considered by the court has been the lack of guarantees in Hungary's legal procedures, both civil and criminal. Under the Communist party, when administrative agencies violated the rights of Hungarian citizens, it was impossible for those citizens to take these agencies to court. The Constitutional Court, however, has declared that those statutes in Hungarian law that prevented citizens from taking legal actions against administrative agencies are unconstitutional. Therefore, it is now possible to have trials against these agencies.

The Constitutional Court has also dealt with many political questions such as elections. Although these have not generally been of great theoretical consequence, there was one case of particular interest worth mentioning. The Constitutional Court overruled a Hungarian law that prohibited Hungarian citizens who were not in the country at the time an election was being held from voting in that election. (This law applied, for example, to people working in Hungary's embassies.) The court declared this law unconditional, but the Parliament (the previous Parliament, before the March and

April elections) overruled the court's decision by modifying the constitution. It introduced into the constitution a measure prohibiting absentee voting. This action was heavily criticized in the press and in journals, and I share with many others the hope that future parliaments will not abuse the constitution by overruling such decisions for purely practical reasons.

What is interesting now is that people in Hungary seem more sensitive to social rights than to basic civil rights. Hungary has extensive freedom of the press and freedom of speech, and all types of viewpoints are represented in Hungarian publications. Now attention seems to have turned to social rights issues such as equality and equal protection under the law. The constitution has a provision for equal protection and also a provision that allows for the possibility of reverse discrimination for those groups of the society who are disadvantaged. For disadvantaged people such as these, reverse or positive discrimination is allowed by the constitution. How to interpret that provision of the constitution is a continuous question before the court. In which case is reverse discrimination, or the granting of more rights to certain groups of people to promote the real equality of those people, allowed? Many people challenge this idea. For example, widows who have three children have exemptions from income taxes. Some people think these parents should have to pay full income taxes, and one argument is that a widow might have a boyfriend; therefore, there is no reason for her not to pay taxes. Those kinds of arguments were rejected by the court because it didn't want to have to investigate people's private lives.

Finally, there are cases regarding the right to life and the right to human dignity. These cases involve capital punishment, which was abolished by the court last October, and the abortion cases, which are pending before the court. These are two very difficult issues that the court must decide.

QUESTION: Does an attorney in Hungary have to meet any special requirements before he or she is allowed before the Constitutional Court? Also, do you know how many attorneys qualify for this status each year?

MR. PACZOLAY: That is a very important question because the court at this moment is divided on that issue. Hungary has not yet fixed the rules on how citizens and lawyers can appear before the court. The court is now working only on written materials and the discretionary right to have oral hearings. When oral hearings are held, sometimes private individuals will be invited to the court, and they will develop their arguments. One of my special areas is to develop the rules of procedure for the court, and another is to make studies on comparing different systems for judiciary review to provide some options to the judges.

Personally, I would like to restrict the number of lawyers allowed to appear before the court to only those who are now qualified to represent citizens before the Supreme Court. I would also like to limit the number of citizens appearing before the court because in certain cases anyone can have a claim before the Constitutional Court. As it is now, however, almost all lawyers can represent before the Supreme Court. Only those who have not passed some special exams or who have no private offices or partners are not allowed to represent before the Supreme Court.

It is difficult to say how many new lawyers are admitted each year because just this year Hungary has basically revised its system regarding attorneys and other legal representatives. Previously, lawyers in Hungary represented either private persons or corporations, but not both. Now, however, Hungary has adopted a corporate law system like those in all other civilized countries. Anyone who has passed a special exam, fulfills certain requirements, and has space for an office can be a private lawyer and can represent both private persons and commercial organizations in civil and commercial cases.

I don't know the number of lawyers. I do, however, know the number of judges. There are 1,200 judges now in Hungary, which is not that great a number.

QUESTION: I have two questions concerning local government. First, to what extent does the constitution grant autonomy to local government? Second, are conservative parties more strongly represented at the local level than at the national level?

MR. PACZOLAY: Before last summer, when new regulations concerning local governmental authority were passed, Hungary's former system of local government was the "soviet" system. Now, local governments (meaning the villages or the districts of a big town) have their own authority and jurisdiction in all matters. Only income taxes and some of the value-added taxes are state taxes. All of the other taxes are levied by the local government. These tax revenues are the income of the local governments and the financial base of their independence.

The second level, which was the transmission from the center authority to local government, is now canceled. Hungary has only eight supervisors who represent the government. Eight regions of Hungary have a kind of supervisor, and in some cases they are the appellate forum from the local governments in administrative cases. Otherwise, they do not control or direct the local governments.

The local elections were held last fall, and the result was a victory for the opposition parties—the Free Democrats and the Young Democrats (not the Socialists). Thus, most local governments now have a liberal majority, and only in a very few cases is the government in the majority on the local levels.

The government says that now the opposition can see and experience what the responsibility of governing entails and how difficult it is. So now they are working quite constructively together. This situation is good for the opposition, which one has to consider as a critic of the government.

QUESTION: Is there any legal procedure for the restoration of property for people who fled from Hungary during the German and Russian invasions?

MR. PACZOLAY: How to compensate those people whose property was appropriated by the state in the 1940s is not the only question. Whether those people should be compensated by the state is the bigger question and probably the most difficult one in Hungarian politics and in the courts today. The government had a bill that would give back to people the exact land they owned in 1947. The year 1947 was chosen because that was the year when the Smallholders party won the elections. The Smallholders party has only one issue now, which is to give back the land to the former owners. This area is their only interest; otherwise, they have no idea about politics at all.

They are important, however, because they are in the coalition, and the future of the coalition depends on their decision. The Smallholders party is not particularly attached to the present coalition but instead is open to forming a coalition government with anyone. This places the other two parties in the government in a very difficult situation because while they are not in favor of returning land, they want to have the Smallholders party remain within the coalition.

QUESTION: Is the president of Hungary a member of the Smallholders party?

MR. PACZOLAY: No, the president is a member of the Free Democrats party, but he was a member of the Smallholders party in 1956 because that is a historical party in Hungary.

The Constitutional Court has said to give equal portions to all former owners. I believe the court will compensate the former owners in some way, but it will be very difficult to do so with the present economic situation of Hungary. It will be a great burden on the Hungarian economy to compensate those people. The compensation issue can also raise other issues. For example, was it constitutional to appropriate the land from the aristocrats in 1945? All of these smallholders had lands that were appropriated from the great aristocratic estates.

NARRATOR: We often talk about transitions as taking place at the highest political level, and political theorists develop theories as to how these transitions should happen. You have told us how Hungary's transition has affected the people and the legal system of that country.

As you were discussing the dilemma of how to treat former members of the Communist party, I am reminded of an experience that I had in Germany of leaving a certain professor's office and subsequently being told that the professor was a Nazi. It had a demoralizing effect. It was confusing for foreigners because we had no idea how to evaluate such statements. For the local population, such statements planted deep suspicions in their minds, and it required a decade, if not a generation, to begin to work one's way through it. While the atrocities of the Nazis made such distinctions essential at that time, your approach to resolving Hungary's conflicts with its past seems much more promising.

MR. PACZOLAY: Deciding how to treat former members of the Communist party is difficult. If Hungarians are serious about living under the rule of law, then they have to decide that from now on the country will not prosecute people because of their past. They should see all people as having the same rights and as legally equal, even those who were Communists in the previous regime. Of course, this is a hard decision morally, but I think Hungarians shall make it and not investigate the pasts of everyone. Hungary has to begin the rule of law sometime, and it should start now.

NARRATOR: We thank our guest, Peter Paczolay. We hope that he will visit again soon and that the transition in your country is successful.

CHAPTER SEVEN

Identity Crisis in the Czech Republic*

VLADIMIR REISKY

NARRATOR: Professor Allen Lynch, the White Burkett Miller Professor at the Miller Center, will introduce our honored colleague, Professor Vladimir Reisky.

MR. LYNCH: Professor Vladimir Reisky was born in Czechoslovakia in 1923. When Nazi Germany occupied his country, the Germans confiscated his family's property outside of Prague, the property of his father, Baron Alfred Reisky de Dubnic, and expelled his family from their home. After the war, the property was restored to the family, but with the Communist coup of February 1948, the property was confiscated again when the Communists seized power in Czechoslovakia.

In that year, Vladimir escaped to England and began to work for the BBC in London. The next year, he received a fellowship to study at the University of Chicago, where he then received both his master's degree and Ph.D. in political science. In 1953 he became an instructor at Harvard University. He has also taught as a visiting professor at Catholic University of the University of Rio de Janeiro in Brazil.

Professor Reisky joined the University of Virginia faculty in 1964 where he remained professor of government and foreign affairs for more than a quarter of a century, retiring in 1990. He

---

Presented in a Forum at the Miller Center of Public Affairs on 23 March 1993.

remains active and affiliated with the university through his directorship of the Institute for East-West Studies, which is based in his family's castle outside of Prague, and which runs a regular summer program for students from this and other universities. Vladimir has also been a consultant to the Institute for Defense Analysis, and in an informal capacity, a consultant to the White House during the Carter administration.

He has been a prolific author in the field of comparative political analysis. His first major work, *Communist Propaganda Methods in Czechoslovakia* (1958), provided a framework for anticipating the eventual collapse of the Communist regime in Czechoslovakia. He is also the author of *Romania and China: From Cooperation to Alliance* (1974). As an indication of his breadth, however, he has also published a book on political trends in Brazil in the late 1960s during his tenure as a visiting professor in Rio de Janeiro. In addition, he has published books and articles on Brazil's foreign policy regarding nonalignment.

It is with great anticipation, Vladimir, that we look forward to your talk today, "The Identity Crisis in the Czech Republic."

MR. REISKY: I recently returned from a two-year stay in Czechoslovakia, where I refamiliarized myself with the contemporary Czech scene. A year after I arrived in Czechoslovakia, the country was falling apart, so I decided to give a talk on this identity crisis. There is much less of an identity crisis now; as other problems have appeared, the question of the unity of Czechoslovakia slowly moved into the background.

When I had to shorten the title of my talk to "The Czech Republic," I was reminded of the story of a diplomat who, shortly before World War II, had to give a talk entitled "Peace in Our Time." He thought about the title and decided he couldn't use it. Eventually, he settled on simply "Our Time."

For the second time in this century, Czechoslovakia has disappeared from the map of Europe, this time of its own volition. This caused psycho-political problems in the Czech lands. In 1989 the Velvet Revolution repossessed the political culture of the pre-war Czechoslovak state, but paradoxically, it lost that state three years later. There was nothing on the horizon to compensate for that loss.

Full membership in the European Community or NATO were only remote possibilities. The historically most natural prospect for an association was Austria, but that country was not interested, for this association could endanger its prosperity, just as East Germany's joining with West Germany has threatened West Germany's prosperity. The Czech dream of joining the family of a united Europe was dissolving, for such a family does not yet exist. President Vaclav Havel, however, very much believes in this dream. He once said that the Czech-German problem will be solved because one day Europeans will all have European citizenship. I think they will wait a long time for this change to occur, but I hope one day he will be right.

The demise of the Czechoslovak state is likely to have strategic repercussions. Is the creation of two small successor states, the Czech Republic and the Slovak Republic, a prelude to a new arrangement of the Central European geopolitical space? Power vacuums are quickly filled in that area of the world. Only an early enlargement eastward of the European Community (EC) or a creation of a Central Eastern European confederation could prevent the area from becoming a sphere of German influence.

The economic consequences of the dissolution of Czechoslovakia will, in the long run, have little adverse effect on the Czech Republic, for it was the relatively rich Czech lands that subsidized Slovakia. In the short run, however, the current 50 percent drop of Czech exports to Slovakia may hurt the Czech economy.

My thoughts are now with Russia, where the possibility for civil war exists. It is a historic time, and obviously the Czech Republic is watching the situation closely. What takes place in Russia will affect it significantly.

What events of 1992 caused the relatively quick liquidation of the Czechoslovak state? I recognize three primary ones:

1. The Slovak nationalists won the 1992 elections in Slovakia. Their objective was sovereignty of the Slovak state.

2.   The Czechs were ideologically too inhibited by the concept of self-determination of nations to embark on a massive campaign against Slovak independence.

3.   The Czech leadership realized that the Slovak economic price for remaining in the federation would be high. They also realized that an early divorce would be less costly than protracted negotiations leading nowhere, or worse, leading to civil unrest or perhaps even repetition of what occurred in Yugoslavia.

In 1968 the Communist regime decided to change the state system of Czechoslovakia from a unitary one to a federal one. The federal structure became a way station for the Slovak nationalists on the way to full independence. But under the Communist centralized system of rule, the adoption of a federal constitution represented more of a gesture than a meaningful devolution of powers to the two constituent states. In Communist-dominated countries, the Communist doctrine didn't have any appeal. To generate some interest in the state, the regime embraced certain nationalist currents and gave the Slovaks autonomy, which made the Slovaks a little more content for a while. When freedom from Communist rule came, this constitution became a time bomb for the self-destruction of the Czechoslovak state. The makers of the Velvet Revolution of November 1989 made the cardinal mistake of not abolishing the Communist federal constitution. They could have abolished it in the wave of enthusiasm for freedom during the first few months, but they didn't. The question is, why? They didn't do so because there is a certain bureaucratic streak in Czech behavior. They said, "We have to preserve some basic laws. We're going to change the constitution, but now we have other things to do." They wanted to maintain a sense of legal continuity.

The liquidation of the Czechoslovak federal state appeared to be an irrational act accomplished by rational means. President Havel tried unsuccessfully to save the federation by way of a plebiscite. The plebiscite was never held. The Parliament was against it, as were the Slovaks, because they would have lost. The dissolution of the country came about by agreement among the major political parties. Negotiations proceeded in a rational, orderly manner, and the country became extinct on schedule. The successor states divided the federal assets at a ratio of two to one, the key being the population distribution: ten million Czechs and five million Slovaks. The Czechs could not very well oppose Slovakia's quest for self-determination, for Czechoslovakia herself was founded on the Wilsonian principle of national self-determination. Woodrow Wilson was the godfather of the Czechoslovak state. The country was ideologically still a Wilsonian state, even after the Cold War.

Created in 1918 as a product of the Versailles peace treaty, Czechoslovakia became a successful democracy. In the perception of the Slovak nationalists, it was an artificial state, for there was never a Czechoslovak nation. The other artificial product of Versailles was the creation of the new state of Yugoslavia, which has tragically disappeared from the map through a vicious civil war. The world has witnessed the collapse of two systems: the Yalta order, which divided Europe into two spheres of influence, and the Versailles system, which was buried twice and in part resurrected after the end of the Cold War.

The death of Czechoslovakia should not cause a serious identity crisis among the Czech people, for the Czechs have a long history of their own statehood. They have tried to explain to the world that they are actually 1,000 years old.

The Czechs had their own kingdom, the Kingdom of Bohemia,* as early as the 10th century. The world was hardly conscious that the Czech Kingdom lasted for 1,000 years, because for the last 300 years of its existence, it constituted a part of the Austrian Empire. When that empire collapsed as a result of Austria losing World War I, the Czech Kingdom also ceased to exist. The Czech crown became irrelevant to the Europe of 1918.

Tomáš Masaryk, the founder of Czechoslovakia and its first president, wrote during World War I that the Czech question was either an all-European issue or it was not a question at all. What

---

Bohemia derived its name from the Celtic tribe of the Boii, who settled in the area in the 5th century B.C.

he meant was that the Czechs had to stand for universal causes to play a relevant role in Europe. President Havel, by stressing the principles of human rights, has given the country a universal cause and thus has made the future of the Czech lands more relevant to the world.

The country's independence was always fragile. In the 70 years of its existence, Czechoslovakia was independent for only 20 years. Since the end of the Austro-Hungarian Empire, the Czechs became victims of two foreign powers and experienced seven different forms of state: the Czechoslovak Republic, the German Protectorate, the Republic of the National Front, the Communist Regime under a unitary state, the Communist Regime under a federal state system, a democratic regime of the Czech and Slovak Federal Republic, and finally, the Czech Republic. A society experiencing seven different systems in the span of one human lifetime must be beset with feelings of uncertainty. The citizen is tempted to ask: What will the next system be, and when will it replace the current one? The relative ease by which foreign hegemonies were established over Czechoslovakia diminished the sense of national pride. But the crisis of identity surfaced only last year, perhaps because the death of Czechoslovakia was self-inflicted.

What happens to values at times of fundamental changes in society and state structure? People tend to cling to the old beliefs. In times of traumatic change—as in the dismemberment of a state—when reality compels them to abandon their beliefs, they may either embrace traditional values, which were held in the times of the genesis of their country, or they may search for new values. Both old and new values have the appeal of not being the root of the current crisis.

In societies intending to behave rationally, the development of coexistence and a balance between traditionalism and progressivism is the norm. This balance might become the case in the Czech lands. If one goes too much to traditionalism, where a situation similar to that in Iran may occur, the end is fundamentalism. If one goes too much to progressivism, the country is disrupted, identity is lost, and equilibrium is prevented.

As the Czech sovereign state has existed since January 1993, there should be no further identity problems, because according to

112

the logic of existentialism, it exists. One would also assume that a people with such a rich history would quickly overcome the identity crisis caused by the dismemberment of Czechoslovakia.

It appears, however, that another crisis is also looming. President Havel, in his first address to the Czech parliament after assuming the presidency of the new republic, observed that many people experienced "a feeling of vacuum."[1] Is this feeling primarily due to the death of Czechoslovakia, or is it a phenomenon of exhaustion resulting from the accumulation of tribulations the country went through? Two quantitatively different feelings of void seem to have converged in the Czech lands. One caused by the death of the Czechoslovak state is not serious because the new country's spirit—the Czech Republic's spirit—will be raised. The other feeling of void is caused by the feeling of spiritual emptiness and moral decay resulting from 40 years of life under the totalitarian regime and also under Hitler. These totalitarian regimes left great scars. Under the Communist rule, this vacuum was prevalent in society, only no one was permitted to talk about it. A Czech official gave a witty answer to one of my students during our seminar's briefing at the Prague Castle. The student asked why there were suddenly so many problems in Czechoslovakia. The official responded: "Under communism, the country's problems were locked in a freezer. When the freezer was opened and the fresh air of freedom melted everything, things began to deteriorate." One might add that Slovak nationalism was one of the frozen packages locked in the freezer.

Symptomatic of the psychological unpreparedness for the dismemberment of Czechoslovakia was the debate in the Czech lands as to what name the future Czech state would have. Pavel Tigrid, a prominent political figure, suggested that the future Czech Republic keep the name Czechoslovakia, for Slovaks were also living in the Czech lands. It was suggested in academic circles that the new state should be named Česko, a name that would sound strange abroad, more like the name of a corporation like Nabisco than of a state. The Čechy, which is used colloquially, was not liked by a professor of Czech history at the Charles University, who felt that "this name is fixed historically to the monarchy."[2] One could not revert to the historical name Bohemia, for geographically it does not include Moravia, which is located between the Czech land and Slovakia. (Incidentally, I read a poll not long ago that said about 40 percent of Moravians want autonomy.)

The issue of naming the future Czech state did not dominate the national debate, which was centered around the question of whether the Czechoslovak federation could be saved. Some Czechs felt it was not worth saving, for the Slovaks wanted Czechs to finance their independence. No responsible politician wanted to prolong the agony of uncertainty, and thus an early deadline was set when Czechoslovakia would cease to exist. The people grew tired of the crisis, for there were other pressing issues to be solved. The feeling grew stronger that under current circumstances Czechoslovakia really was an artificial state. To the Czechs, Slovakia seemed to be a political and economic liability. Thus, the mind-set changed in the Czech lands from ardent advocacy of the Czechoslovak federal union to advocacy of a separate Czech state.

After things settle, the new Czech Republic might yet officially embrace the historical name, the Lands of the Czech Crown. An indication of this trend seems to be a passage in the preamble of the new Czech Constitution that proclaims: "We, the citizens of the Czech Republic . . . at the time of renewal of an independent Czech state, loyal to all good traditions of the ancient statehood of the Lands of the Czech Crown. . . ."[3] There is a practical reason that would speak for reverting to the lands' historical name: the question of the permanency of the Czech borders.

The demise of the Czechoslovak state made certain circles question the legitimacy of the Czech borders. A Sudeten German publication stated that, "In terms of international law, the demise of Czechoslovakia means also the end of the territorial sovereignty over the Sudetenland [the border lands of Bohemia settled by Germans].[4] One of the counterarguments would be to point to the 1,000-year-old integrity of the borders of the Lands of the Czech Crown. The borders of the Czech Kingdom were stable. While the Czech lands were a frequent battlefield—as most European countries were—the Kingdom's historical borders were always restored, with the exception of parts of Silesia, which were lost to Frederick the Great. The geopolitical space of the former realm of the Czech Kingdom was spared partition among foreign powers.

114

The contemporary reason for invoking the memory of the historical statehood of the Crown of Bohemia and for the new Czech state considering itself the heir to that ancient statehood was not nostalgia for times past, but rather a quest to reestablish the integrity of the geopolitical space of the Czech lands. One could argue that a historical boundary and a tradition of statehood cannot assure the preservation of the borders of the new Czech state. If the law of the jungle should again prevail in Europe, which it might, then nothing can preserve a small state. In a civilized international setting, however, historical precedent always was, and will be, an important part of international law.

The geopolitical vacuum in Central Europe is a specter that still haunts the minds of people of the area. International and national politics abhor a power vacuum. Thus, President Havel wanted Czechoslovakia to be under the umbrella of NATO. Many Czechs believed that their country—with its history as an integral part of the West—should not have to wait in line for long to become a member of NATO. One can imagine what NATO's aloofness does to the Czech quest to regain a broader European identity. The aspirations of Czechoslovakia, Hungary, and Poland to become members of NATO have all met with negative responses, but lately Washington and Bonn have begun to contemplate the possibility of an associate status for these countries. It is important to recall the 1930s, when Europe's lack of strategic interest in the region led to the abandonment of Czechoslovakia in Munich.

In the 19th century, when Czech aspirations for emancipation were of no interest to the world, Czech historian Palacky had this advice: "In work and knowledge is our salvation." The Czechs followed this advice, becoming the most advanced industrial nation of the Austro-Hungarian Empire. In the process, they found a degree of self-fulfillment and strengthened their national pride. In the first republic, Czechoslovakia ranked as the eighth most developed nation in the world. Palacky's prescription, if followed today, could enable the nation to catch up with Western Europe economically within five to seven years.

Economic progress alone, however, cannot solve the Czech quest for strategic security. The Czech lands were always geopolitically insecure. This insecurity drives the nation to strengthen its cultural identity. From the ashes of Czechoslovakia might rise a new historical consciousness that would strengthen the cultural uniqueness of the Czechs and the legitimacy of the new Czech state. There are parallels with Israel. If Israel did not have its glorious past, its biblical past, Israel would be less important on the world stage. Similarly, the Czechs are turning to their past to enhance their importance because they objectively see how relatively unimportant they are. The emphasis on the historical past is, in today's circumstances, an endeavor for the culture of the nation to survive. The more closely the Czech Republic is integrated economically with its stronger neighbor Germany, the more important it will be for the people of the Czech lands to preserve their identity and uniqueness.

It can be unsettling to the national self-esteem of the Czech citizen traveling abroad when he hears time and again: "You are from Czechoslovakia. That state just ceased to exist. From what part of the country are you, and what is the name of your country now?" Such questions lead the people toward reexamination of the nature of their statehood, which might generate a useful debate of the pros and cons for the Czech lands rehabilitating the historical concept of the Czech Crown.

The danger of destabilization may strengthen the country's awareness of its ancient statehood. There are signs that this is already happening. Significantly, the speaker of the Czech parliament, Dr. Milan Uhde, has handed over copies of letters and other documents of the Czech kings to President Havel on the last day of his presidency of the soon-to-be-extinct Czechoslovak state. At the time of the disintegration of the Czechoslovak state, this act served to remind the public that the end of Czechoslovakia meant also the recommencement of the Czech statehood tradition.

In the 19th century, when the Czech quest for emancipation, its national awakening, began, Palacky coined the motto: "We existed in the past and will exist again." He well understood the importance of the nation's past for the future. Greater awareness of this past would give the state and society a self-confidence necessary for its normal functioning. To be conscious of the nation's roots is particularly important today when everything is in flux. Central and Eastern Europe seem to be afflicted by contrary

116

currents: integration versus disintegration, democracy versus anarchy, material progress versus economic crisis, moral revival versus valueless existence. Small nations could be paralyzed or could even disintegrate by an aggravation of these contradictions. Remembering the political roots of the nation is an important part of "damage control." The Czechs would weaken the concept of their own Czech statehood by continuing to bemoan the demise of Czechoslovakia, which, being pragmatists, they've stopped doing.

There are two indicators from which one can assess the health of a society: the material and the spiritual. It is much more difficult to take a measure of the latter. Materially, the ten million Czechs are relatively well off in comparison to the other countries that were under the Soviet Empire. When one looks at the nation from the spiritual perspective, one can see a cultural continuum, but also an interrupted value system.

National identity cannot be found exclusively in the spirit of Masaryk's republic or in the ethos of the historic Crown of the Czech lands. Rather, it must be found by drawing on the best of both traditions. But even that is not enough. The Czech state and society must also be innovative. To survive, a small state must also be relevant to the rest of the world. To paraphrase Masaryk, the Czech search of identity should also be seen as a global rather than as a parochial problem. The current crisis in the Czech lands is not unique; it mirrors the world's lack of spiritual cohesion. The world is no longer what it was, and it is not yet that what it is going to be. The way the Czechs overcome their crisis might yet inspire other nations in similar crises.

This is not to say that the Czechs are more qualified than other nations to peacefully solve social and political problems, but it is perhaps good to recall that it was the Czech and Slovak innovative concept of 1968 that started the ball rolling toward the disintegration of the Soviet Empire. Their concept of "socialism with a human face" was co-opted 20 years later by Gorbachev. To go further back in history, the Reformation in continental Europe had its genesis in Jan Hus, the Czech professor of theology at Charles University. Thus, the Czechs are a small nation, but they are rich in ideas. It will be good to watch what conceptual and practical consequences they draw from their current identity crisis.

MR. LYNCH: The political result in Czechoslovakia after 1989 is the same as in Yugoslavia and the Soviet Union; that is to say, the disintegration of a previously Communist multinational federal state. In all three cases the political results are the same in terms of the integrity of state structure.

Yet there are very different outcomes in terms of the degree of civil violence in all three cases, with Czechoslovakia being the most peaceful case, Yugoslavia being the most violent case, and the U.S.S.R. being somewhere in between. Outbreaks of civil violence and war have occurred on the periphery of the former Soviet Union, while there is still substantial peace reigning between the main, predominantly Slavic, populations that constitute the core of the former Soviet Union.

Why is there peace in the Czech case, war in the Yugoslav case, and something in between in the Soviet case? Is it a question of the state of democracy, democratic institutions, or traditions? Is it a question of the relative homogeneity of the populations in the Czech lands as compared to the Slovak lands, taking into account the Hungarian minority and the Ruthenian minority also in Slovakia?

MR. REISKY: There are several factors. Perhaps the factor of greatest importance is that Slovakia never had any enmity toward the Czechs. As a result of World War I, the Slovaks and the Czechs lived together under the Austro-Hungarian empire and were liberated at the same time. So, the Czechs and the Slovaks got together. They were never enemies. On the contrary, in the 18th century the Slovakian tongue had fallen into disuse. They used to read Czech books to prevent themselves from being Hungarianized. The Slovaks were a Slavic people who had a certain affinity to the Czechs.

Masaryk didn't invent Czechoslovakia by just sitting in Washington and saying, "How should I make Bohemia bigger?" He knew that the Slovaks had nowhere to go after they declared their independence from Hungary. The Hungarians today still call Slovakia "Upper Hungary." Can you imagine what is going to happen if the Hungarians ever get strong? Thus, the Slovaks, having nowhere to go, were very happy that Masaryk had this

118

conception of a Czechoslovak state. He was born very close to Slovakia and knew the Slovaks, so they joined forces. The result, a unitary state, was a fairly happy arrangement for the Slovaks.

This whole history is very different than, for example, the nations of the Caucasus that were clobbered by Russian imperialism. The Slovaks never suffered under the Czechs. On the contrary, the Czechs were constantly pouring money into Slovakia, so there is absolutely no reason for the Slovaks to take up arms against the Czechs.

QUESTION: The remnants of the Austro-Hungarian Empire now comprise as many as ten nation-states. It would seem from what you say that there is only a minimal chance for stability with this kind of a background, particularly since the economic status of many of these nation-states differs greatly.

Is it too much to hope that many of these states could be brought into the EC? Or, is there any possibility that some sort of a federation—let's say an Eastern European Economic Community— could be formed with these people? Are the antagonisms and the nationalisms such that this possibility wouldn't work?

MR. REISKY: There is no antagonism against Austria today. When President Havel was in Austria on a state visit, he said it was a co-responsibility of the Czechs and the Austrians to stabilize Central Europe. He has a vision of strong cooperation or co-responsibility with Austria. One would have to drag Austria into a confederation because Austria has today the best of two worlds: It wants to remain neutral as well as be a part of the European Community. One has to encourage Austria to get more involved. Havel is doing precisely that with his diplomacy.

QUESTION: How about Hungary and Bulgaria?

MR. REISKY: Bulgaria is a little bit too far away from the Czech Republic, and there have never been any ties between Bulgaria and the Czechs, except in early Christendom when Bulgarian bishops came to Prague. But there are really no cultural ties, and since

Bulgaria was not part of the Austro-Hungarian Empire, nor were there historical ties.

All of these ideas of a central European federation remain only a remote possibility. A durable federation must arise from the grass roots. The people of Austria will have to want a federation, and the people of other countries will also have to want it. If only the statesmen get together and make such an agreement, it will again be an artificial union, no matter how good the idea.

COMMENT: The policy of the British government is to integrate Poland, Hungary, the Czech Republic, and presumably Slovakia anyway, into the European Community and NATO as quickly as its partners will allow. So far the British government has not been able to persuade its fellow members to agree, either about NATO or in the EC. This policy of bringing the Czech Republic, Poland, and Hungary into Western Europe as quickly as they can arrange it is, I think, not an impossibility.

MR. REISKY: I think such ideas of integration are extremely important, especially in view of what is happening in Russia today. The West can again be involved in a cold war in no time if the Russian military or some Russian imperialists take over. It is extremely important that these gains in freedom be consolidated. It would be terribly shortsighted on the part of the West not to take some of these countries into NATO. The moment is auspicious; it might be too late in five years.

QUESTION: What became of the strong defensive rampart system that I remember reading about at the time of the 1938 Munich agreement, which was then Czechoslovakia's bastion of defense against Germany?

MR. REISKY: That system is gone now. When Hitler overran Czechoslovakia, he took all of these armaments because the Czechs were armed to the teeth; they were ready to resist. Then came Munich and the whole borderline was dismantled because Hitler first took the Sudetenland. It was precisely in the Sudetenland where these fabulous fortifications were similar to France's Maginot

Line. There were underground cellars with weapons stored, and there were other fortifications such as antitank bunkers. At Munich this was all given to Hitler on a big silver platter.

QUESTION: In the search for Czech identity, would it make any sense for the Czechs to consider Switzerland as a model? Like Switzerland, the Czechs are part of Europe, yet stand a little apart. Also, the Czech Republic has various ethnic and linguistic groups, as does Switzerland.

I also have a second question. Is there any sign of a backlash in Slovakia? Is there a more sobering side to their independence?

MR. REISKY: As far as Switzerland is concerned, in the two years I recently spent in Czechoslovakia, not one person presented a Swiss model. In contrast to the Swiss, I think the Czechs were always part of a broader Europe. For example, they were part of the Holy Roman Empire. The Czech kings were electors of the Holy Roman Empire. They felt themselves to be Europeans.

Among the Czechs there is a strong desire for integration into Western Europe, whereas Switzerland is more aloof. They don't like to be integrated into anything. They think they can stand on their own. The Czechs know they cannot stand on their own. For this reason the Swiss model cannot apply, and no one raises it.

As to your question on whether there is a backlash in Slovakia, the backlash is coming surprisingly early and is quite strong. There is a strong backlash against Meciar, who is the prime minister of the Slovak Republic and who led the dismemberment. For example, the minister of economics resigned, and Meciar had a big fight with the foreign minister. I am sorry to say, because I have nothing against the Slovaks, that they are behaving like a banana republic. They are learning, perhaps, but the biggest danger is that if the Slovaks continue like they are, they will have an authoritarian system, because Meciar wants to curb the criticism of the press, among other things. But I doubt that Meciar will get away with such authoritarianism because the resistance against him is growing already.

MR. LYNCH: On what is the resistance based?

121

MR. REISKY: It is based on the economic situation. If Meciar were to get a big loan from the Germans, all Slovaks would say, "Bravo! We are independent, we will have a good standard of living, and we will surpass the Czechs." But he did not succeed in obtaining strong foreign economic support.

The Germans have a wise policy. When Meciar was in Bonn, he tried to pin down Kohl by saying, "We have to have a special relationship," and that special relationship meant money, of course. Kohl rebuffed him because the Germans have good relations with the Czechs and don't want to spoil that relationship.

QUESTION: In regard to the European Community, for a long time, Germans were distinctly unpopular with Czechoslovakia because of Germany's wartime occupation. Now that the situation is resolved, how are they going to get along now or in the future?

MR. REISKY: The Czechs are flexible people; they tend to quickly forget. They are attracted by the economic power of the Germans. They know that the major investments are coming from Germany. There is even a sort of morbid joke being told that when they were discussing what name the Czech state should have, someone said, "Why not call it East Germany?" To my tastes, however, the Czechs somehow cater a little too much to the Germans. For example, in Prague one will only find menus in the German language in the plush restaurants these days, so I think it is the attraction of money that talks.

The Czechs are very pragmatic; they say that Germany is now a democratic country, so why not? Obviously, if some resurgence of Nazism occurs, the Czechs, with their humanitarian beliefs, would change their minds about the Germans, but at the moment, the mood is extremely positive toward the Germans. After all, it is Bonn and not the East Germans who are running Germany. The East Germans are rather dangerous people in a sense because they were not yet democrats.

MR. LYNCH: That was always Adenauer's view, and one of the reasons he resisted unification.

MR. REISKY: He was right. If any trouble is forthcoming, it will come from the east, from Prussia.

QUESTION: Could a further problem arise with the Hungarians, or at least the people of Hungarian ancestry, in Slovakia, wishing to have their own autonomy?

MR. REISKY: Yes, but the Czechs say they don't have anything to do with this situation; if the Slovaks are punished for undoing Czechoslovakia, they will suffer. If the Hungarians do something to them, the Czechs are not going to defend them because they asked for independence. The Czechs didn't want Slovakia to be independent; they wanted to have a common army and they would defend Slovakia, but now they really don't care.

QUESTION: How do you account for the expulsion of about three million Germans from Czechoslovakia at the end of World War II, when the real ties of the Germans who were expelled were largely to the old Austro-Hungarian Empire?

MR. REISKY: This is an extremely complicated and emotional question with the Czechs. I think Havel, who is a tireless defender of human rights, thought this action was a great injustice toward the Germans, but he doesn't pursue it because a political backlash would result. In other words, theoretically Havel felt it was inhumane to expel three-and-a-half million people, some of whom were children and young people who had nothing to do with Nazism. But if Havel takes an ideological position, some Sudeten Germans will say, "You are taking an ideological position. Now you have to take step number two, which is, when are we going to get our property back?" Havel would have to reply, "Never!" Havel is interesting; he is not only an ideologue, but a statesman as well. He knows that if he said he would give the Sudetenland back, the Czechs would not like it at all. The Czechs consider it a kind of war prize for the fact that Germans lost the war.

QUESTION: At one time Paris and Prague had a close relationship. Is that tie still strong?

123

MR. REISKY: It seems that it is gone forever. It has been this way since about 1938. After Munich, the Czechs said that if the French deserted them in the 1930s, they would desert them again. There are cultural interests, yes, but not political interests.

QUESTION: Haven't the French attempted to reestablish such political relations?

MR. REISKY: Perhaps, but the attempt is more on the cultural level. The French, however, may be playing a stronger political card with Poland. The Czechs have only 10 million people, whereas Poland has 39 million people. So, in case of some trouble in Europe, the French are trying to have closer relations with Poland, and they also hope the Czechs will go along. From the Czech side, there appears to be no interest to form a political axis.

MR. LYNCH: I might note, and you can certainly correct me, that the French had actually abandoned Czechoslovakia several years before Munich; that is, the construction of the Maginot Line committed France to a purely defensive strategy against Germany, thereby nullifying its alliance with Czechoslovakia, which could only be effective in the event that France would take the offensive to protect Czechoslovakian interests in the event of a German aggression. That issue had long been settled, and Munich simply codified that reality.

QUESTION: Is there a solution to these problems we have been addressing, or are these issues perhaps insoluble?

MR. REISKY: Disintegrative forces are now at work all over the world. It can be seen in Canada, in Spain with the Basques, and so on. This kind of disintegrating force can be ascribed to nationalism.

The answer is that there is no real common language between various nationalists. There is no unity of spirit, no moral unity. If there were some moral unity, one could curb that nationalism. In other words, the only thing that can override these disintegrative forces is an appeal to universal moral values, such as to the French Canadians or the English-speaking Canadians. After all, people have certain moral values, so let's pursue them, and this will bring people together again. If there is any long-term answer, it is to have young people be more interested in moral values in order to keep a kind of unity of the Western world.

MR. LYNCH: I would like to address the issue of public spirit, which may relate to moral values as well. J. F. Brown, one of the most perceptive observers of Eastern European politics, has worked for Radio Free Europe for many decades. In a chapter in his book on Eastern Europe published in 1987, he argued very forcefully and persuasively that there was a severe loss and perhaps even a death of public spirit in Czechoslovakia because of the frustration of the lack of alternatives for public expression, particularly as the changes in the Soviet Union and elsewhere in Eastern Europe were beginning. The perpetuation of the "normalization" of Czech politics following 1968 and the appointment of Mr. Yakeš as the first secretary who helped to organize the seizure of the airport as the head of Czech counterintelligence had the effect of channeling what would have been perhaps public energies into private energies. How far off was he in 1987?

MR. REISKY: I think he was pretty well on the mark because the Czech state was broken in 1968. In 1968 they had hoped to disengage from Soviet totalitarianism and establish some mild form of socialism. The crackdown by the Soviets broke their spirits, and made Czechoslovakia feel impotent. A tremendous demoralization, which is still present, has occurred since then.

If East Germany hadn't collapsed, Czechoslovakia would still be Communist today because the Czechs absorbed what was happening around them, helped by the small underground led by Havel and a few intellectuals. The workers didn't pay any attention to politics, so there was no mass movement. Then the situation was one where the Russians were telling the Czech Communists not to shoot the Czechs if they demonstrated. The Russians said they were neutral. The Czech Communists suddenly became frightened when they saw what happened in East Germany, and they folded. There was no bravery on the part of the Czech underground; they did not confront the Communists with weapons. Instead, the whole thing collapsed. Then Havel and a few students emerged from the underground, but they had no program. They had to quickly organize a government, but they were not prepared for it because it had happened so fast.

So Brown was right. In fact, there was such demoralization that students had to go to factories during the Czech liberation week in November 1989 and try to persuade the workers to take to the streets. The workers asked why and asked if they wanted to repeat 1968 with the Russians coming again. They didn't know that the Russians were so decimated. Only the intellectuals knew that the Russians were so weakened and thus began to regain courage. There was, however, tremendous demoralization.

MR. LYNCH: In effect, then, even the restoration of Czech independence was primarily attributable to external factors and not internal factors.

MR. REISKY: The country was eager to be independent internally but didn't believe it could be, so in reality, I would say that the force was external.

MR. LYNCH: Thank you, Professor Reisky, for gracing us with your presence and thoughts today. We look forward to seeing you again soon.

Vladimir Reisky

ENDNOTES

1. *FBIS*, 24 February 1993, 6.

2. *Lidove Noviny*, 24 July 1992, 9.

3. *Constitution of the Czech Republic of December 16, 1992*, published by the Czech News Agency (CTK), Prague, 18 December 1992.

4. *Deutscher Ostdienst*, a bulletin of the Sudeten Germans published in Bonn, cited in *Lidove Noviny*, 15 September 1992.

CHAPTER EIGHT

Eastern Europe:
Free Countries—Captive Press*

GENE P. MATER

NARRATOR: Gene Mater is vice president of the International Media Fund, a private, nonprofit organization involved in developing independent media in Eastern Europe. He served in the U.S. Army's psychological warfare branch in World War II. He then became a reporter for several newspapers and news director for Radio Free Europe in Munich. He joined CBS in 1970, becoming a senior vice president, and served as CBS representative to the European Broadcasting Union and the Asian Broadcasting Union. Mr. Mater also helped found the North American National Broadcasters Association.

He is now retired and lives in Charlottesville. He does consulting work and is interested not only in Eastern Europe, but also served as a member of the U.S. Commission on Broadcasting to the People's Republic of China. It is a pleasure to welcome Mr. Mater.

MR. MATER: Democracy is on trial again in Central and Eastern Europe, and this time it is not doing too well. These new democracies are failing to protect some of the basic freedoms the West had hoped would flourish, particularly freedom of the press. A quick overview of the emerging democracies in Eastern Europe

---

Presented in a Forum at the Miller Center of Public Affairs on 5 March 1993.

illustrates the following common faults with the print and broadcast media and with journalists themselves.

First, with regard to the print press, most newspapers, including the independent ones, are printed on state-owned presses in state-owned publishing houses for distribution by state-owned agencies. It gives the state in these countries an inordinate amount of active or potential control. Moreover, many of the larger dailies are owned by the state, political parties or movements, or other special interest groups. As a result, people with political power frequently attempt to control the newspapers' content. Broadcasting has fared worse than the print media. In all countries, the goal is basically the same: prime ministerial or presidential control over what is broadcast, generally with a fair degree of success. Finally, the journalists themselves may represent the saddest part of this equation. Today's generation of journalists has spent a lifetime under one repressive regime or another during 40-odd years of communism. They are typically uncertain about their role, their relationship to government, and their responsibility to their audience.

In Slovakia, for example, some members of the Slovak Journalists' Syndicate have formed an offshoot group called the Journalists for a Truthful Picture of Slovakia. Their real mission is to play it safe with the new authoritarian government. In Hungary, I met recently with the leaders of a similar group who had formed a separatist journalist association. When I asked why they took that action, they replied that they thought there already was too much press freedom in Hungary. We reached an impasse when I asked how they quantified freedom.

Lest anyone thinks I'm the only one who holds a negative opinion about the press in Eastern Europe, let me refer to a few newspaper clippings that will provide a better foundation.

> When President Iliescu of Romania sees a news item he doesn't like on Romanian television, he sometimes picks up the phone and has the story killed or altered in mid-broadcast. In Budapest a legislator recently denounced Hungarian television's weather broadcast for continually

forecasting dry, sunny days. Such forecasts were depressing the country's farmers and must be stopped.

Washington Post

State fires more journalists and other Slovak opposition voices silenced.

Prague Post

Slovakia's Uncertain Dawn: With the government tightening its control over the press and television, opposition politicians and some journalists have stepped up their attacks on the democratic credentials of Prime Minister Meciar.

International Herald Tribune

Three years after the collapse of communism, journalism has been reinvented in Eastern Europe as a craft involving independence and objectivity, but politicians remain uneasy and sometimes ruthless about the new press freedom.

New York Times

We don't want press freedom because it is a besmirching freedom. We want honesty of the press.

Hungarian journalism professor and well-known writer

A *Washington Post* op-ed piece called "The New Crop of Dictators" was about the fight for control of the electronic media and the press from Budapest to Warsaw, from Bratislava to Zagreb. Finally, on 14 February, the *New York Times Magazine* ran an article titled, "How Milosevic Stole the Election in Serbia" about Milosevic's control of Belgrade radio and television.

As an interesting aside to illustrate Milosevic's control over the media in general, the International Media Fund tried to help Studio B Television, an independent station in Belgrade. Last December it sent them studio equipment from the United Kingdom worth $236,000. It was able to take it only as far as the Serbo-Hungarian border; there were no flights to Belgrade. The studio's truck picked up the equipment, but it was hijacked about 50 meters into Serbia by men in two black limousines. We have not seen the equipment since then, or the truck, for that matter. There is no great Serbian interest in free broadcasting.

All of the articles I have quoted sound extremely negative, and while they accurately illustrate the situation, there are still pockets of independence and hope. Let me describe the situation in some of the Eastern European countries with which the International Media Fund deals, offering a little of the good and a little of the bad. In so doing, it might be worth remembering that the Virginia Bill of Rights of 1776 carried this wondrous sentence: "The freedom of the press is one of the great bulwarks of liberty and can never be restrained but by despotic governments."

Poland has had its own form of democracy for almost four years, including a relatively free print press. Broadcasting is another matter, however. President Lech Walesa said that he is keeping four portfolios under his control: military, police, foreign affairs, and broadcasting. Still, a broadcast law that legalized independent stations was finally passed by parliament last December and was signed by Walesa in late January, three-and-a-half years after Poland became a democracy. Actually, this measure was taken in self defense. Currently, in independent-minded Poland 46 pirate radio stations and six pirate television stations are on the air, so there is some hope that this law might be able to regularize the system.

The broadcast law itself is far from perfect. As a broadcaster, I might add that the U.S. Communications Act of 1934 as amended is also far from perfect. The Polish law has some troublesome aspects, however, such as a section requiring programs to support certain (undefined) Christian values. The mechanism to license stations is still being set up, so the outcome remains to be seen.

The former Czechoslovakia offers some of the best of the good and some of the worst of the bad. I'll treat the two republics as the independent countries they now are. In the Czech Republic, publishers are taking over newspaper distribution. Removing distribution from government control can only be a positive step. The newspapers themselves are in a state of transition; mergers and failures are commonplace, but they are the result of market forces rather than of repression. Still, even people like Václav Havel have tried to exert pressure on newspaper editors regarding content.

While it was still unified, Czechoslovakia enacted the first broadcast law in Eastern Europe. After the separation, the new Czech Republic quickly licensed 36 radio stations, most of which are on the air without government interference. Prime Minister Václav Klaus, however, recently made some unfortunate remarks about that independence. The law that created the broadcast regulatory agency called for an independent group of nine members, each named for six years. The prime minister now says that he can handle such matters out of his office, so there is no need for an independent agency. He also managed to amend the law to permit dissolution of the independent broadcast council if parliament either fails to accept the council's annual report or fails to approve the budget. The agency's future is thus rather uncertain. If that description appears ominous, it is meant to be.

Most of the larger newspapers in Slovakia are owned or controlled by state agencies, and almost all are printed on state-owned presses. There are a few independent newspapers that are popular. A clear indication of the Slovakian government's role in the print media may be found in what was formerly one of the country's most popular daily newspapers, *Smena*. *Smena* originally was, and legally still is, owned by the Slovak Youth Federation, which is controlled by the Ministry of Culture. Under the direction of a young editor by the name of Karol Jezik, *Smena* became a popular general-circulation newspaper.

Jezik, however, is a little too independent-minded for the new government. In reporting the elections last June that brought Prime Minister Vladimir Meciar to power and assured the breakup of the country, Jezik carried the results on page one—inside a bold, black border. Two months later, verbal attacks on Jezik and *Smena* began, and finally on 4 January 1993, Jezik and the paper's business manager were fired, ostensibly because *Smena* was unprofitable, which is not true. Jezik left *Smena* on 10 January, along with 46 of his colleagues who resigned in protest. On 15 January, they started a new newspaper, *Sme*, that is rapidly becoming as popular as *Smena* once was.

I am pleased to report that the International Media Fund will be providing Jezik with the desktop-publishing equipment he so urgently needs. It will also be assisting two other independent dailies, one in central Slovakia and one in eastern Slovakia. These newspapers are among the few pockets of independence that one can find.

The broadcasting situation in Slovakia is as bad as it is for newspapers, if not worse. The state television news director was fired last fall for not being pro-government, and the same thing happened to his successor early this year. There is extremely tight control of broadcast content. Perhaps the best example of the new Slovak government's attitude will be found in one official's title: state secretary for culture and mass media policy of the Slovak Republic. That title says it all. As for the journalists themselves in Slovakia, Meciar recently urged them to engage in ethical responsibility, which means self-censorship.

In Hungary, the newspapers are not troubled much by government interference, perhaps because, according to the best estimates, 75 percent of the newspapers in that country are controlled by foreign owners, including French, German, Swiss, and even American companies. The broadcasting situation is another matter, however. There are almost no independent radio or television stations in the entire country. There is no broadcast law and no mechanism to license new stations.

The Hungarian parliament met in a 17-hour marathon session this past New Year's Eve in an effort to pass a broadcast law. By that time, the original 68-page draft bill contained nearly 700 amendments from the six parties in parliament. When it came time to vote, not one ballot was cast in favor of the bill, which may have set some sort of parliamentary record. Nevertheless, there were 213 applicants for radio station licenses and 123 applicants for television licenses, so there is still hope that something positive will take place. It is anticipated that Prime Minister Jozsef Antall will unilaterally lift the government moratorium on broadcast licenses soon, so the party faithful can start stations in advance of next year's national elections.

The prime minister has taken two other steps, however, that far surpass the parliamentary disaster. He managed to oust the independent-minded heads of state radio and television, replacing them with loyalists to his center-right government. Far more serious is the fact that a recent law places the state broadcasting budgets under the control of the prime minister's office, effectively giving him a line-item veto on any programming that he finds offensive or with which he disagrees.

Similar problems exist in the other Eastern European countries as well. For example, the head of Bulgarian radio and television had begun to implement a wonderful program for broadcaster independence, but he was voted out of office last week.

I have provided a brief overview, and the revolution obviously hasn't ended. Indeed, in many of Eastern Europe's leaders proof is visible of the old adage that the true ambition of the slave is not to be free, but to have a slave of his own.

Where does one go from here? While I'm not by nature a Pollyanna, for a number of reasons I have not given up hope of seeing a truly free press in Eastern Europe. First, on a personal level, every time I go to Eastern Europe I am reminded that more than 30 years ago when I was the news director of Radio Free Europe in Munich, I was surrounded by exiles broadcasting to their home countries, countries that I visit today. I'm not sure that at that time I really believed I would be walking the streets of a free Budapest, a free Warsaw, a free Prague, or a free Bratislava some day. The brave people of Eastern Europe have created their own revolutions, and now they have to create their own democracies.

Second, my friends in the Eastern European press do not see only doom and gloom, possibly because the situation is far better today than it was four years ago. It is not as bad as some of them had feared.

Third, a major reason to believe that Eastern Europe will see a truly free press is faith in the next generation. Today's youth want more than just a little freedom; they want it all. For that reason, the International Media Fund is devoted in large measure to training and teaching. It has established centers for independent journalism in four cities thus far, and it has journalism programs with a dozen universities in the region, generally in concert with American universities.

Finally, as Americans view events in Eastern Europe, it is important to remember that it took six years from the end of the American Revolution until the United States had its Constitution, and still another three years until Americans had the Bill of Rights. Perhaps it will take nine years for such things to come to pass in Eastern Europe, but I would like to believe that they will indeed occur.

QUESTION: There are many stories in the U.S. press about ethnic strife in this country. It appears at times as though the press is actually fanning the flames of ethnic hatred and driving people apart. Consequently, Americans see more and more violence in their streets. Is the same thing taking place in Eastern Europe?

MR. MATER: With regard to Eastern Europe, most of the countries have laws that prohibit the type of stories and reporting to which you referred, stories that fan the flames of hostility between various groups. The ethnic problems in that region are far more serious than they are here.

QUESTION: You mentioned that President Havel exerted pressure on newspaper editors. Could you give us some examples? If true, it would appear to be a bad sign. If Havel, who is very freedom-oriented, would resort to such an action, then anyone in the United States could also do so.

MR. MATER: During Havel's previous term, when he first became president, his people, including his press secretary, met on his behalf with the newspapers and threatened them. Havel later realized that a mistake had been made and that he had stirred up the people. He offered a quasi apology, but the threats did take place.

There is a belief in Eastern Europe and around the world, unfortunately, that at the time of transition as a new government is formed, the press should be the handmaiden of government and help support it. I totally disagree with that belief. Press loyalties don't change during the transition of presidential administrations in this country. If one looks at the history of the press in the United States, some newspapers attacked George Washington even more viciously than they attacked Clinton, Bush, or anyone else.

NARRATOR: Thomas Jefferson devoted part of his second inaugural address to a diatribe against the press for its irresponsibility. He argued, however, that such excesses are best curtailed by relying on the force of public opinion instead of government censorship. He believed that the truth would triumph in the end if one has faith in the people, but he also suffered mightily from the criticisms. Almost every president does.

MR. MATER: In one of those rare instances during my tenure at CBS, we won a case in the Supreme Court. According to the Court, for better or worse, editing is what editors are for, and editing is selection and choice of material. That editors, newspaper or broadcast, can and do abuse this power is beyond doubt, but that is not reason to deny the discretion Congress provided. Calculated risks of abuse are taken in order to preserve higher values.

QUESTION: Could you comment on whether Radio Free Europe and Radio Liberty are needed nowadays in reinforcing the increasing freedoms of the press and broadcasting in formerly restricted areas? Would similar broadcasts into China be useful?

MR. MATER: Radio Free Europe and Radio Liberty merged a number of years ago when their funding became public and subsequently went through Congress instead of the CIA. The worst-kept secret in Washington was that they were originally funded by the CIA. They now broadcast as one unit. It would be a mistake to close Radio Free Europe now, as President Clinton proposed. It serves as a rather cheap insurance policy that helps in the development of democracies in Eastern Europe. It is a voice that should continue.

The situation in China is different. Last year, as a member of the U.S. Commission on Broadcasting to the People's Republic of China, I wrote the minority report. It was a 6-to-4 vote. The basic issue this commission presented to the White House and Congress was whether Radio Free China should be separate or whether it should be included in the Voice of America (VOA). The minority believed that it should be included in VOA and that VOA should intensify and expand its coverage in China. We did not think it made sense to start a new instrument called Radio Free China or Radio Free Asia. Instead, we should capitalize on VOA's large and loyal audience by increasing the amount of broadcasting, particularly internal coverage.

QUESTION: I was intrigued by your question of how to quantify freedom. While one cannot quantify it, don't people implicitly measure it all the time? The judgment of whether freedom is expanding or contracting derives from experience. It is not merely an abstract issue. It applies to a dynamic socio-political situation in which freedom of the media is not the only value. Governments, for example, have the responsibility to govern, at least to the extent of maintaining order, and avoiding chaos in the economic system. People have to eat. As a result, society has a number of goals beyond maintaining freedom.

MR. MATER: Americans have an ethical heritage that is probably unknown in the rest of the world. The First Amendment, as I understand it, was established to protect the public more than the press. A press controlled by the government cannot be justified under any circumstances. The key to a successful democracy such as the United States has is an informed electorate, not an instructed one.

In the Serbian election, for example, Milosevic controlled both radio and television broadcasting. As a result, every report during the campaign about his opponent, Milan Panic, was negative, and Panic couldn't even buy ads or air time. Unfortunately, Meciar is heading in that direction in Slovakia, as is Antall in Hungary.

NARRATOR: The Bill of Rights and the First Amendment freedoms result, then, in the courts deciding in cases where the public or national interest conflicts with the freedom of communication, instead of delegating the decision to a political authority. The government cannot run the press, but it can bring a case to court.

MR. MATER: More often, public interest groups rather than individuals bring cases. This is what libel laws are all about, and there is nothing wrong with it. From time to time, the press does make mistakes. One example is the recent resignation of Michael Gartner, a First Amendment absolutist, as president of NBC News. A point is eventually reached where one realizes one has gone too far and has made too many mistakes.

One theory, to which I don't completely subscribe, argues that the press has a right to be wrong. They do, but only up to a certain point. When the press begins to fabricate the news, it is a little different.

QUESTION: Does control of the press possibly serve a function that is illegitimate but understandable? In those countries without a tradition of strong party discipline, a truly free press might create a chaotic, unrestrained democracy. Political leaders can see that possibility and therefore resort to using press controls as a means of enforcing discipline.

MR. MATER: There is, in my opinion, far greater political party discipline in Eastern Europe than you suggest. It is actually one of the major problems in some areas. In Hungary, for example, there are six parties in parliament. Very little crossing of party lines to vote for anything occurs, unfortunately, and party control is fairly rigid. As a result, since Antall controls a coalition of three of the six parties, he was able to push through a law that gives him control of the state radio and television budgets. He did it through strong party discipline. I'm not sure that total party discipline, as people are accustomed to seeing in Europe, is the best way to do things. It tends to undermine independent thought. Party newspapers can be found throughout Eastern Europe, just as there were in those brief periods of democracy between the two world wars.

QUESTION: How successful has private external broadcasting been in penetrating the Eastern European markets? I was in Prague at the time of the attempted coup in the Soviet Union. We were able to receive CNN clearly several times a day, even in French and German.

MR. MATER: Jamming no longer takes place. Radio Free Europe used to broadcast almost entirely in shortwave, along with some medium-wave transmissions to Czechoslovakia, Hungary, and Poland. They now broadcast domestically, and they actually have local stations that are licensed. Material from Munich is relayed to Prague, Warsaw, or Budapest, and it is broadcast there. There is access to a great deal of foreign material if the people understand the languages. The BBC and VOA also broadcast domestically in various places throughout Central and Eastern Europe. As a result, people now receive a wealth of information.

NARRATOR: Does it lessen the risk to freedom posed by the government-controlled press if the countries are permeable by outside communications?

MR. MATER: No, as events in Bulgaria illustrate. According to a gentleman I met recently from Bulgaria, the only way to get a true picture of what is taking place in Bulgaria is by listening to Radio Free Europe. The state broadcasters do not provide a clear picture at all; they are run by the government. This situation is likely to continue, since the reformer I mentioned was voted out of office last week.

QUESTION: The journal *Vreme* from Belgrade seems independent and unrestricted. Could you describe its background and status? Also, are there more magazines like it in other Eastern European countries?

MR. MATER: *Vreme* is independent, and the International Media Fund has helped it by providing some desktop publishing equipment. I don't know its history because most of my traveling is in the northern tier of Eastern Europe. I haven't been to Yugoslavia in 30 years. There are other magazines similar to *Vreme* in the former Yugoslavia, Serbia, Hungary, and elsewhere.

140

QUESTION: Do journalists in Eastern Europe debate the issue of press freedom versus responsibility the way people do in the United States?

MR. MATER: I'm sure they do. When I worked for CBS, on a number of occasions I met with journalism students at various universities around the country. Questions like yours arose often. How far does one go? How wrong can someone be? Frankly, we were probably the best protected at CBS. We had our manual of news standards and practices. CBS was also the first network to appoint someone devoted solely to news standards who had access to everything that was taking place.

Did that practice mean that we didn't make mistakes? No, because there is always a human factor. Unfortunately, a reporter may look at a story and decide he can do better if he changes this or that excerpt, and often no one is looking over his shoulder. Theoretically, the only way I know of preventing all of the problems in television would be to have a duplicative second staff that would check everything that was done at every step, including sources. An attempt of this nature to eliminate problems would create an almost impossible situation.

NARRATOR: One of the ways that the difference between straight reporting and editorializing has come to be recognized in the last decade is the increased use of the news analysis label on an article. Don't the editors themselves still exercise a fair amount of control over the internal rules in each news organization?

MR. MATER: I was a newspaper reporter before I became a broadcaster, and I come from the old school that doesn't believe there should be any mixing of opinion and news. The news story itself should be as straight as humanly possible. Unfortunately, that is a foreign concept for most of Eastern Europe and occasionally for some of my brethren in this country.

QUESTION: I find your remarks very interesting, and I am familiar with the work of the International Media Fund. There is much to be done in Eastern Europe, especially in those countries

141

that still have authoritarian governments. You are to be praised for your efforts.

I sense that you may have wanted to say a bit more about the successes. Maybe you would like to comment on the leading papers in the areas with which you work, such as the *Gazeta Wyborcza* in Warsaw. How would you gauge their level of reporting? Since it is not a government paper, my own impression is that it would be unfair to group it generically with the unfree government-controlled press. How does its circulation, which equals 12 percent of the Polish population, compare to that of leading U.S. newspapers such as the *New York Times*? In addition to the *Gazeta Wyborcza*, there is *Polityka*, which is a weekly newspaper that appeals to intellectuals but also reaches some 7 percent of the Polish population. *Mlada Fronta Dnes* in Czechoslovakia and the *Nepszabadsag* in Hungary are other examples.

I would also like to comment on Yugoslavia. Some of the most brilliant journalism that is being written in the world today originates in Belgrade and Sarajevo. *Vreme* was mentioned as one example. *Borba*, which is also printed in Belgrade, is extremely responsible, informative, and sometimes downright brilliant. I can remember one headline written by a young man who was reporting from Sarajevo: "If war is the answer, what is the question?" What is your impression of these newspapers?

MR. MATER: One of the things that the International Media Fund has been doing, particularly with newspapers, is conducting various training sessions. There is a complete lack of understanding of the duties, responsibilities, and relationships that newspapers have, not only with the public, but with the government itself. It preaches the separation of news and opinion. Taught primarily by American newspaper reporters and radio broadcasters, these sessions explain how an independent newspaper, radio station, or television station should function properly.

There is still a great deal of uncertainty about the role of the press vis-à-vis its audience and the government. One of the training sessions, for example, concerns the relationship between the press and the government. When I began working in the Czech Republic, I met with someone who at that time was applying for, and since has received, a license for a radio station. He offered this hypothetical question: "What do I do if the mayor of my town, a town in northern Bohemia, gives me a story that I know is not true? If I broadcast it, the people will know it is wrong. What do I do?" First-year journalism students deal with these types of questions. Freedom is an acquired taste and not something that can be fully understood via classroom lectures.

The newspapers that you mentioned are doing well. On the other hand, *Mlada Fronta Dnes* in Prague sold 49 percent of its ownership to the French. I don't know if that sale affected the journalistic quality of the paper. I argued with the paper's editor about his reasons for making the sale; he did so because he needed the money—he received $20 million. Sales of this type are taking place throughout Eastern Europe. Currently, the Czech Republic is investigating 27 newspapers in Bohemia and Moravia that are owned by one German newspaper.

The International Media Fund, in contrast, aims to develop an indigenous media. It has a basic rule that if foreign investment in a project is more than 20 or 25 percent, it will not become involved. The situation is changing drastically for newspapers as well as broadcasting. The Czech Republic recently licensed a private television network which is 70 percent owned by Americans and Canadians and 30 percent by a Czech bank.

COMMENT: There is the dimension in Eastern Europe of a struggle for freedom. You witnessed it while you worked for Radio Free Europe, and it has been taking place for many years. In other words, along with 40 years of communism, there was also a long struggle by intellectuals to gain their freedom. Some of those intellectuals have produced brilliant journalism.

In the case of Belgrade, the problem is not to educate the people in *Borba*, *Vreme*, or Studio B Television about the meaning of democracy. They are intellectuals who risk their lives facing an authoritarian regime. There, it is somewhat of an old-fashioned struggle between the good guys and the bad guys.

I realize that the International Media Fund is working diligently on an important aspect of Eastern European freedom. I mentioned these points to counteract any impression that there aren't brave, gallant, and brilliant journalists still at work in Eastern Europe.

MR. MATER: Absolutely, and Karol Jezik in Bratislava is a perfect example, as is *Slobodna Dalmacija* in Croatia.

QUESTION: Are assertions of First Amendment rights becoming excessive? For example, in the case of the World Trade Center bombing in New York, the story broke before the FBI wanted it to. The FBI had a suspect but did not want to arrest him; instead, they wanted to follow him so as to find the other conspirators. When the story leaked, however, they had to arrest him.

MR. MATER: Whether one is talking about that story or any other case where the press has supposedly done something wrong, one has to bear in mind that the story came from someone. In the case of the World Trade Center bombing, for example, it was obviously that someone told the press about the suspect, possibly the FBI.

It isn't a question of the press seeking these things. The reporters who stood on the beach with the lights and cameras when the Americans landed in Somalia did so because they were told it was where Marines would land, so they assumed they were expected to go and take pictures. Similarly, there is nothing irresponsible about the fact that the press ran the story about the bombing suspect because someone gave it to them. The point that people must remember is that someone is giving out these stories, and whether it is the White House or the FBI, they all do it.

NARRATOR: There are cases in which the president has called the publisher of the *New York Times* and made a special request for a delay or a suppression of a story in the national interest. There is nothing the president can do if, in the *New York Times'* judgment, it is in the national interest to publish the story. A request from the FBI to a local reporter, however, is not likely to be received in quite the same way as a call from the president to a newspaper publisher.

MR. MATER: The *New York Times* did delay a story on planning for the Bay of Pigs operation. They had the story and knew what was going to occur. President Kennedy called and asked them not to carry it, and they complied. The President later said that the biggest mistake of his life was asking the *New York Times* not to carry that story. Things would have been better had it been made public. The operation probably would have been canceled.

QUESTION: Has the International Media Fund received any hostile reactions to its efforts?

MR. MATER: No, I don't know of a single instance where there has been any hostility toward our efforts, at least publicly. What happens behind closed doors, however, I don't know. Still, no one has posed a problem, and so far we have been quite successful.

NARRATOR: We are delighted to have had Mr. Mater share with us his experiences and insight on press freedoms in Eastern Europe. He has reminded us of the fundamental value of a liberty people too often take for granted. Thank you very much.

IV.

CHANGE AND REVOLUTION

CHAPTER NINE

Principles of 1989: Reflections on Revolution*

STEVEN LUKES

NARRATOR: When the story of this university is rightly told and the focus is drawn to the level where the work is done, Ralph Cohen will be very much at the center of that story. He is the director of the Center for Literary and Cultural Change at the Commonwealth Center, and it is through his good graces that the Miller Center has been put in touch directly with Professor Steven Lukes. I have asked Professor Cohen if he would be willing to introduce Steven Lukes, and he has kindly consented to help. It is an honor to have both of you.

MR. COHEN: It is a special pleasure to be able to introduce Steven Lukes. No one who has read his books could possibly fail to realize the philosophical temper of his study of both sociology and politics. From 1964 to 1966 he was a research fellow at Raphael College, and then from 1966 to 1988 he was a fellow and tutor in sociology and politics at Balliol College, Oxford. He is now professor of political and social theory at the European University Institute, Florence, Italy.

MR. LUKES: The essay is an attempt to answer the following question: What were the revolutions of 1989—some of them successful, some unsuccessful—in the name of? Some may think it

---

Presented in a Forum at the Miller Center of Public Affairs on 18 April 1990.

is a mistake to try to generalize across the cases of Hungary, Poland, Czechoslovakia, Tiananmen Square, Romania, even Bulgaria; but that is what I'm going to try to do.

I want to focus on something that has been almost completely neglected by students of the communist world, social scientists, and kremlinologists. The neglect of this dimension in part helps to explain their total failure not merely to predict what occurred last year, but even to foresee the possibility of what occurred last year. Indeed, until the beginning of last year, it was an orthodox belief that most of what happened was systematically impossible. What has been neglected is what one might call the moral dimension of political behavior. The demoralization of the governing elites was an important aspect of the story of what occurred last year. Morally motivated actions likewise played an important part in these events.

I want to address two questions. First, what was the prevailing political morality of official communist societies up to the period of the revolutionary transformations that occurred or in some cases are in the process of occurring? Second, how can one interpret these transformations? That is to say, in the name of what were these regimes rejected and overthrown?

The first question may seem odd to anyone who is struck by the decay of Marxist-Leninist ideology in the societies of Eastern Europe and the cynicism, corruption, and generally manipulative character of the ruling elites. I certainly don't mean to suggest that these regimes remained legitimate in any strong sense; that has not been true for a long time. Nevertheless, it is possible to say that there was an official political morality in the sense that public discourse was dominated by a certain mode of thinking and a certain political vocabulary, which were propagated on television and in the schools. The whole ideological apparatus continued to function even though belief in the content of what was being propagated had disappeared in many, though not all, places. The degree of belief in the official morality differed from regime to regime.

In a wonderful essay on the power of the powerless, Václav Havel gives a very good description of how a greengrocer puts into his window a little sign that says "Workers of the World, Unite!" Havel then asks a marvelous question: Why does the greengrocer put that sign there? Clearly, he doesn't believe that workers of the world either have united, are uniting, or are likely to unite, nor does anyone passing the window believe in this prospect. Havel proceeds to analyze the pressures at work that maintain the form of the belief while the content is gone. As someone once said to me in Czechoslovakia, it is as if the discourse of official Marxism-Leninism was a kind of noise that blocked out other forms of thought and expression and simply by occupying the area of public discourse prevented the development of alternative ways of thinking and talking. Broadly speaking, this was the way in which Marxism continued to exist until last year. I believe there are and always have been certain features of Marxism as a way of thinking and a way of talking that could be identified as being the constitutive features of the political morality of Marxism-Leninism as such. By "political morality" I mean the structure of thinking that determines one's values and the political judgments that one can and cannot make if he or she holds and speaks that language and adheres to its tenets.

What distinguishes Marxism as a political morality is that it is a morality of emancipation promising universal freedom from the peculiarly modern slavery of capitalism through revolutionary struggle. It makes a promise. It promises a world of abundance, cooperation, and social rationality with the free association of the producers, whose common relations have overcome egoism in full collective control of the natural and social world. Thus, the idea is that freedom is a long-term goal. The questions of how to behave, how to act, what policies to be pursued—Lenin's famous question, What is to be done?—are always to be answered by a kind of futuristic question of what is going to bring about or bring nearer the leap into freedom. I think this feature of Marxism was very well identified in a sentence by the Austrian Marxist Ernst Fischer, who said:

> Only the future is interesting, the fullness of what is possible, not the straitjacket of what has already been, with its attempt to impose on us the illusion that, because things were thus and not otherwise, they belong to the realm of necessity.

151

From the perspective of Marxism, certain facts and features of the world that people might think to be necessary, are rather thought of as historically contingent; to suppose them to be necessary is simply to cling to an ideological fiction blocking human progress. I would identify four such "facts" that I think Marxism holds not to be necessary to the human condition or to all societies. I shall call them the facts of scarcity, particularity, pluralism, and limited rationality.

"Scarcity" is in one sense a simple notion that means limits to desired goods; however, there are different kinds of scarcities. There are scarcities of natural resources relative to production. There are scarcities of consumer goods relative to consumer demand. There are also scarcities that are rather more complicated that result from limits of space or limits of time. There are other scarcities that have to do with the very nature of the goals people seek; for example, we cannot all have high status. Marxism has an inherent promise of overcoming scarcity, especially regarding natural resources and consumer goods, in a world of abundance. This promise has always been a major tenet in Marxist thought.

By "particularity" I mean the fact that human beings are motivated, properly so, by a whole range of different concerns: commitments to one's family, religious community, region, friends, or nation. People are also motivated by concerns that are more abstract in form: for example, the belief that people should be treated in certain ways just because they are human beings. These kinds of concerns lead people to give to charity, follow rules of justice, or respect the rights of strangers. I think that Marxism, like certain other moral positions such as utilitarianism, requires people only to be motivated by abstract concerns, in particular the abstract concern for the well-being of future generations. In other words, Marxism expects of people that they will only be motivated by the interests of the future of humanity, or else it says that people should be motivated by class loyalties in the belief that these classes are going to be transformed or abolished through the class struggle.

By "pluralism" I mean the existence of fundamentally divergent conceptions of what matters in life, of what John Rawls has called "conceptions of the good." I mean that these divergences are not eradicable; one cannot expect a future in which the differences

152

between different cultural and value positions are going to disappear. In other words, one will have to accommodate to a world of fundamental differences of value. Marxism denies this notion. It attaches no importance to the existence of particular religious, ethnic, national, cultural, or political divergences. It believes that in the world of the future, these will disappear.

Finally, by "limited rationality" I mean limits on the capacity of human beings in real time to solve certain problems, or to do so without creating other problems that undermine their solution. This is deemed by Marxism not to be a necessary fact; full, rational control of the natural and social world are within human grasp. This is the Promethean belief in the possibility of the total domination not only of nature, but of human nature and social life.

Marxism denies that these facts are necessary. It denies that people must accommodate to them and learn to live with them. It argues, on the contrary, that people can, as Ernst Fischer says, imagine the world otherwise and bring a world about in which these facts can be overcome.

What does it mean to regard them as necessary? I think it means that if people take scarcity, particularity, pluralism, and limited rationality to be facts with which they have to live, then people will recognize the need for principles of justice for the regulation of social life. These are what Rawls calls "the circumstances of justice" that face the citizens of any conceivable society of a certain complexity. In other words, conflicts of interest will arise involving a distributive struggle owing to the fact of scarcity. Conflicts of interest will arise out of the fact that people are inevitably and will forever be motivated by different concerns that have different scope—some more particular, some more abstract. Conflicts of interest will result from different values and different fundamental beliefs about what matters in life. Differences will arise because there is no correct and rational solution for every problem and because differences of view about what the right thing to do are going to exist forever. If one says all of that, if one accepts that these conflicts of interest will not be overcome, then one is going to say that he or she will need principles of justice. One will need, in other words, to consider the importance of having a set of principles for the distribution of benefits and burdens and for the assigning of rights to protect interests and corresponding obligations.

My central argument has been that Marxism has always been inhospitable to drawing these conclusions, essentially because it regards all of these conflicts as the pathologies of pre-history, and in particular as stemming from the anarchic production relations and class conflicts of capitalism. It believes this in part because it takes the facts of scarcity, particularity, pluralism, and limited rationality to be contingent and not necessary. In a word, I think Marxism has no place for considering the importance of justice and the centrality of rights just because it regards these necessary facts as not necessary.

But surely, it might be said, Marxism has a powerful moral message, and Marxists have had an honorable place in countless struggles against injustice and against the violation of rights. I think that objection misses the point. Of course Marxism has offered to victims of injustice and oppression and to those who sympathize with these victims an inspiring vision of a future free of both injustice and oppression. The objection that Marxism after all is a moral message misses what the inspirational core of that message is. What inspires those who grasp what Marxism promises is not the prospect of a complex, conflictual, and pluralistic world regulated by principles of justice and the protection of rights, but rather the overcoming of the very conditions that require such principles and protections. It is the prospect, in other words, of a world in which justice and rights, together with class conflict and the oppressions of the state, will have withered away. Communism has promised an end to injustice and oppression, but it didn't promise justice and rights. It promised, rather, emancipation from the enslaving conditions that make justice and rights necessary. In other words, communism is a world beyond justice and rights.

Now I want to come to what I think happened last year. In the name of what political morality did these revolutionary movements take place? Of course, a proper answer to this question would require serious and detailed academic study of all of the available evidence, suitably weighed for its importance. In advance of that, it can safely be said that these revolutionary movements were at one on at least the following five points.

154

First, they were citizens' movements actively invoking the idea of citizenship. In virtually every case, appeals were made by citizens that entailed stepping back from more particular and immediate commitments and interests. Hence the rhetoric of "round tables" and "forums," especially in Czechoslovakia and East Germany, was new in, among other things, just this respect. The students of Tiananmen Square were seeking to transcend their generational and occupational identity and speak in the name of the people. From mid-May the demonstration expanded to over a million people, including workers, party bureaucrats, professionals, and even units of the military. One of the slogans shouted in East Germany was "We are the people." People could argue about what it meant, but I think that among other things, it meant just that the definition officially given of the people was no longer acceptable. The point I'm trying to make is most dramatically made by the Timisoara uprising, which originated with the protest of Hungarian Protestants. However, these protests and particular demands of Hungarian Protestants were not what that demonstration was about.

Secondly, these were movements for distributive justice and fairness. They were protests against the arbitrary allocation of advantage and opportunity and against failed command economies that were themselves a major source of scarcity as well as injustice. In general, they were protests against a system governed by no rationally defensible distributive principle. Of course, there wasn't much agreement about what distributive principles would be just, only that free capital and labor markets should play a key role in these economies' transitions: Even demoralized, departing political elites agreed on this point. The most important question for the future is what role government intervention in these economies will play in ensuring more just distributive systems.

Third, these were defensive movements, and this aspect is one of the things that makes them so interesting. They were revolutions for procedural justice, the rule of law, the protection of basic constitutional rights and liberties for the individual—the Principles of 1789, as distinct from the positive social and economic rights that were added to these by the Universal Declaration of Human Rights in 1948. These movements were directed in part at abuses and corruption by individuals (Ceausescu, Honecker, Zhivkov) and by

155

a whole political class, as in China. However, the principle motivation of these movements was the rejection of an entire institutional system that worked through command, was restrained only through bargaining, and whose official rationale lay entirely in the future it promised rather than in its responsiveness to present individuals' interests.

There was one particular individual right that was of special significance in 1989: the right to free travel across frontiers. It was the mass exercise of this right by East Germans and its subsequent recognition by the state that unleashed events in East Germany and thus all that followed. The right to leave one's country is, as Locke intimated, a right of peculiar significance, for only where it is effective can the according of consent to a regime or a system be a genuine choice. Clearly, Egon Krenz, in opening up the Berlin Wall, supposed that doing so would be a founding act of legitimacy for the East German regime.

Fourth, these movements were pluralist movements. They demanded an end to the monopoly of power, the *nomenklatura*, the euphemistically described "leading role" of the party, and the "ghost parties" and false "alliances" playing roles based on frozen statistics from the past. These movements demanded an end to the suppression of local, regional, and national issues and to the suppression of the real histories (as in the Baltics) of how nations were incorporated into the Soviet Union. They demanded an end to the denial of expressions of ethnic and religious identities. The revolutions stood not only for the expression of pluralism and diversity, but also for the value of these principles.

Finally, these movements were skeptical: not only of the content of what socialism had promised materially and morally, but also of the very cognitive pretensions of the parties who had lost their way and abandoned any serious claim to knowledge-based, let alone science-based, authority. This skepticism is, in part, obviously a result of the massive economic failure of the prevailing systems, and the justifiable doubts as to the prospect of reforming them from within. This skepticism, however, is representative of a more universal trend: a new sense of the complexity and uncertainty of the interaction between man and nature and an awareness of the adverse ecological consequences of the old Promethean Marxist

156

vision of ending human exploitation through the exploitation of nature.

In sum, these were revolutions against the hubris of individual leaders, political elites, and an entire political class. They were also revolutions against the hubris of arbitrary and oppressive economic, social, and political systems whose claims to legitimacy were no longer supported by the proclamations of their rulers. Above all, they were revolutions against a political morality that for decades sustained these systems and their leaders. In this sense, one could say they were revolutions of fallen expectations and revolutions in the name of freedom, but of freedom, in a sense Hegel never intended, as the recognition of necessity.

COMMENT: Maybe what should be emphasized is the fact that America serves as a model for a realistic utopia, in contrast to the absolute utopia of Marxism. In America, the idea of justice is seen as an adjudication of evils, whereas Marxism promises to abolish evil.

MR. LUKES: Yes, America is a model, as was dramatically demonstrated with the Statue of Liberty in Tiananmen Square. However, perhaps a certain skepticism should be retained about the idea that this occurrence was simply some kind of triumph for western liberalism. I would rather be more neutral, because for one thing, what people know and understand about America in Eastern Europe is very partial and very colored by their hopes.

The story is a complicated one. There are residues, after all, of the old communist systems that people don't want to throw away. I think people are very contradictory about this matter. For instance, there is the question of rights: What kind of rights did people want to protect? I think among these are the welfare rights and the socio-economic rights which, despite all of their faults, these systems actually provided. Although it is true that writers like Hayek are very popular among intellectuals, I would be surprised to find much support for the dismantling of the welfare state that taking this country as a model would actually imply.

COMMENT: It is clear that this is not a monolithic kind of movement. There are varying degrees of commitment to a free-market system in the Eastern European countries. It depends on which parties one talks to.

MR. LUKES: Just to talk for a moment about specifics, I was in Hungary recently and spent quite a bit of time with some of the leaders of the Free Democrats. Of course, the Free Democrats didn't do terribly well in the last election, but I think the Free Democrats are themselves what one might call the social democratic component, which is actually quite important among the leading intellectuals and the leading members of the party. For very good reasons, however, this aspect is not given much emphasis in the election campaign, because clearly the priority right now is to reintroduce both the political market and the economic market. If I were of the left wing in Hungary today, I would argue for the reinstitution of the free market because that is the only way to move toward a more egalitarian society in the end. Thus, even within the Free Democratics, the picture is not so clear.

QUESTION: Do you think that the impoverishment of the majority in these countries had much to do with the revolutions, especially since they were aware of the prosperity of the capitalist countries?

MR. LUKES: I do think that in part these movements were rebelling against poverty, but it is not just impoverishment. Ever since Tocqueville, people have known that impoverishment doesn't bring about revolution; it is rather the recognition of relative deprivation. This observation brings up the interesting question of when and how things became sufficiently apparent. It became apparent to people that the system had failed, and the promises, including the economic promises, couldn't be kept. I don't believe, however, that this sense of deprivation relative to the capitalist states is enough to explain the revolutions. I think that perhaps Solidarity in Poland was the crucial historical turning point, and there both a sense of injustice and deprivation were the main motivations.

QUESTION: Isn't time very important in this issue? One can ask people to accept injustice or ignore the question of justice for a period of time if there is a greater goal to be reached. It seems as if any reformist regime, however, whether Marxist or not, has only a limited amount of time to achieve its goals.

MR. LUKES: Yes, I agree with that thought. Of course, the question of why it lasted so long is then raised.

COMMENT: In Czechoslovakia it lasted so long because the people had become used to leading a double life under the Nazis and even under the Austro-Hungarian empire. The leaders selected to implement Marxism were certainly uneducated and were put in by the force of the Soviet army. There was this disdain for the leadership during the whole period on the part of the intellectuals and the students who created their own intellectual and social lives.

MR. LUKES: I agree with much of what you say, and the writings of Havel and others have given a fascinating analysis of that area. Someone once called it the ideology of "as if": One behaves as if he or she believes, like the greengrocer, and one has this extremely elaborate system of a dual life. However, I disagree with your assertion that the early Marxist leaders were uneducated. The early Bolsheviks and even later generations were led by the crème of the intellectuals, and in Czechoslovakia after 1948 the intellectual elites, almost to a man and to a woman, apart from those who left, supported the regime. Even until quite late, a significant part of the intellectual class were in support of it.

QUESTION: I was under the impression that the "utopia" of free markets played a large role in inspiring these revolutions. What do you think of this idea?

MR. LUKES: That is an interesting and alternative interpretation—in other words, it's not Rawls, it's Hayek. I'm saying that these movements are really for pluralism, justice, a recognition of diversity, and the need for principles to regulate conflicts of interest. The alternative view is that what inspired them was another utopia,

159

the neoliberal utopia. I'm sure evidence can be produced for each view. I do not doubt that economic liberalism has very popular advocates in Eastern Europe, not least among them some of the advisers of Gorbachev. I don't think this economic liberalism was a dominant aspect of the movements last year, although there are powerful tendencies in this direction, as can be seen, for instance, in Poland and in the economics ministry in Czechoslovakia. This is just one trend among others, however, and even now countertrends can be seen within these governments. It is a powerful movement among intellectuals, but I don't think it is the whole story.

QUESTION: How well can Marxism be compared to the medieval church, which created a bureaucracy for its own corrupt purposes? Could these revolutions be seen as a modern Reformation?

MR. LUKES: I like that analogy somewhat. It is actually one, if I recall correctly, that was drawn long ago by Leszek Kolakowski. Like any analogy, it is an imperfect one, but I think there is something in it. What separates Marxism from religion, however, is that the eschatology is an earthly one. The promise it offers is something that is actually supposed to be on the historical agenda. Unlike Catholicism, unlike "real" religion, so to speak, Marxism doesn't have many consolations to offer, only promises.

NARRATOR: I wondered about your conclusion regarding hubris. Isn't that intimately linked with the "hard utopia" that is scientifically confirmed in Marxist thought? If there is certainty on this earth of a hard utopia, then isn't one justified in his or her hubris? It isn't merely the ordinary corruption of leaders by egoism; it is the ultimate corruption in that one knows one is absolutely right. For example, if you are Stalin you know that your goals justify sacrificing five million kulaks. In a dialogue between Stalin and Lady Astor, he asked her how many people were destroyed in automobile accidents in the West, and to what end? He then stated that in Russia the destruction of the kulaks and others is toward a very clear end. The eschatology and political religion defines and confirms that in every way.

MR. LUKES: Yes, it did have this religious quality. A marvelous passage in Lev Kopelev's memoirs describes how after engaging in the liquidation of kulaks, which he did as a young Communist, he came to the realization that the whole structure of thinking in which he had been raised contained no resources within it with which to resist or question what was being done. The way of questioning it was to summon from religion or memories of other traditions the means of moral resistance.

What is interesting to me is the way this has continued to have an impact lately in the form of demoralization. I don't think people had much of a religious attitude to Marxism in Eastern Europe for the last 20 years. It did not have that kind of religious appeal anymore. In my trips to Eastern Europe over the last 10 or 15 years, I would ask people if there were any true believers left, and people found it difficult to find any. Once in Warsaw, I asked a friend staying there, "Are there any true believers left?" He said he had a friend who was and that he would invite him for breakfast the next day. This person came, and he was a very nice young student doing his thesis on Marx's theory of the concrete and the abstract. At last, I thought I had found a true believer, only to find that he had actually switched his thesis study from Marx to Edmund Burke, whose concreteness he particularly appreciated.

My main point is that the structure of thought of Marxism, which is essentially inhospitable to the language and thought of taking justice and rights seriously, continued to operate even though the faith had gone. I think that is what the revolutions were about, the reintroduction of that whole framework of thought.

QUESTION: One of the successes of liberal thought has been in incorporating opposition and criticism into its own paradigm. What is the prospect of Marxism doing that? Now that the form is gone, do you see any hope of the content coming about?

MR. LUKES: I agree with you about liberalism. Liberalism is a kind of permanently absorbing creed. I used to give a seminar in Oxford with Ronald Dworkin called "Liberalism and Its Critics," and I was endlessly struck by the way critics of liberalism somehow became liberals, and by the way in which people in the class would make objections to Dworkin, and yet within a week he would incorporate what he saw as valid in their critiques. That is an interesting feature of liberalism as a system of thought.

Marxism doesn't have this degree of flexibility. On the contrary, what has happened with Marxism is that although it has some very profound aspects to it, as a structure of thought it is finished. There is one old cliche that states "We're all Marxists now." People can say that without meaning that they accept the structure, but instead they accept particular aspects of Marxism: For instance, the way in which Marxism has entered into historical studies is that fragments of Marxism become incorporated. It may well be that in 20 or 30 years people won't be using quite the same categories.

QUESTION: I wonder if you would say something with regard to the dangerous rise of nationalism and anti-Semitism in Eastern Europe. Could you also comment on the valuable role of the church in affecting the revolution in Poland?

MR. LUKES: As well as being pluralist movements, these were also plural movements in that they incorporated many elements, some of which are really not very savory and certainly not very pluralist. It is a paradox that if one has pluralist movements, that doesn't mean that all of the elements of the movement are going to be pluralistic. Some of them are going to be rather anti-pluralist, and the task for a civic-minded pluralist movement is to deal with the non-pluralist components of the whole.

In Eastern Europe, this is being tested. In Hungary it will now be put to the test because I think the party that won the recent elections has demonstrated, especially in some of the speeches of its leaders, some very worrying antipluralist tendencies, both nationalistic and anti-Semitic. I can only say that this is the great problem for the future in Eastern Europe: the growth and the power of movements that are really quite threatening to what the revolutions promised.

As for the church, I think that as always, the Polish church played an ambiguous and cautious, although historically very important, role in these events. And it has been playing such a role all along. It is obvious that in Solidarity different tendencies of the church were at work. The church itself, I would say, has been playing a pluralist role, incorporating and continuing to value the diversity of different tendencies.

QUESTION: I think that one can see three very distinct tendencies within these revolutions: first, the neoliberal or free market stand; second, a social democratic component; and third, a very formidable and dangerous nationalistic current tending toward the precapitalist, feudal past. Would you say this is an alliance of three very different movements?

MR. LUKES: I would. I agree with that statement, but I would also say that what was distinctive about these revolutions was that they were movements that represented all three, and at least for a time represented the value of the diversity of the three.

NARRATOR: Where are the forces of moderation? Where are the forces of accommodation with the capacity for mitigating conflict and acting as a poultice to draw out some of the infection and rivalry? On the one hand, intellectuals have a well-praised quality of balancing truth and looking for the center of moderation; on the other hand, intellectuals have been notably unsuccessful in playing the role of moderator. Among American foreign policymakers, Chip Bohlen was a much better diplomat than George Kennan was, for example, and yet Kennan was far better as a thinker and historian. What does this prevalence of intellectuals in the movement mean in terms of controlling the conflict?

MR. LUKES: I wouldn't be very hopeful about intellectuals. If one looks at the history of intellectuals in relation to Marxism and communism in the West, the story is not very encouraging. It is difficult to generalize about intellectuals as a stratum, because the character of intellectuals differs, but I wouldn't be particularly sanguine about intellectuals as a source of hope. One such source may be Gorbachev himself, because it seems that he is very aware of his status as both a precipitating and facilitating factor in this whole story. Of course, one man, however crucially placed as he is,

163

is not going to be enough to stem these dangers of which you speak. There are powerful forces in some of these countries—for instance Czechoslovakia—that are a source of encouragement. I think that the dangers of nationalism, specifically Slovak nationalism, in Czechoslovakia are not so acute; it is not a society where anti-Semitism has ever had any deep roots. Poland and Hungary are different, and there, I think, are real dangers ahead. Eastern Germany is a very mixed story. I don't share the most alarmist views about the dangers of German reunification.

QUESTION: Will the key to the success of these revolutions be the countries' abilities for economic development?

MR. LUKES: Yes. This is a whole other subject, but it seems to me that the West, and in particular Europe, should take a much more global or coordinated view than it does. The great virtue of the Marshall Plan was that it took a unified view of the problem and said to the various countries involved, "Look, you've got to cooperate in order to do this. We're not going to decide where this aid is going to be spent; this is actually a political problem that you've got to sort out." The unification of Germany makes this much less likely as a strategy, but there are tendencies—for instance, Havel's proposals for various regional associations between the states of Eastern Europe. I think that the West should do absolutely everything possible to encourage those movements.

NARRATOR: Well, we have had a rich intellectual feast. We are grateful to all of you, and we hope that Professor Lukes will come back in the future.

CHAPTER TEN

Central and Eastern Europe: Unfinished Revolutions*

DANIEL N. NELSON

"Unfinished Revolutions" urges a mid-course correction in U.S. policy toward post-Communist Central and Eastern Europe. It does so responsibly, carefully, and with due consideration to the limits on external influence over a vast region in which populations' hopes and fears are unlikely to be swayed by Washington, D.C. decisionmakers.

But in adjusting what Americans try to do in and for Europe's eastern half, we should practice zero-based policy-making . . . setting aside long cherished assumptions, for example, about the synergy between democracy and the free market, and about the capacity of "free market democracies" to be self-sustaining.

In "Unfinished Revolutions," the target for U.S. and Western policy is support for economic reform in post-Communist Europe. The Working Group acknowledged the interplay between political and security realms that affect such reforms. Nevertheless, the sights of this Policy Paper are set squarely on the considerable problems of systems undergoing the wrenching shift from state ownership and central planning to an economy driven by market forces.

Unstated but assumed is the capacity of market economies to reinforce democracy and, over time, to foster peace and stability in a region. U.S. and Western assistance that provides effective

*Reprinted from a policy paper series, January 1993, Rozanne L. Ridgway and John P. Hardt, co-chairs.

support to reform is thus regarded as feed for the horse that will pull ahead the cart of peace and prosperity.

But this causal chain is weak at every link. In the wake of revolution lies post-euphoric postcommunism, in which systems are distributed along a continuum that ranges from proto-democratic to neo-authoritarian. The region is, furthermore, rent by strife varying in severity from full-scale conventional war to intermittent strikes and governmental instability. This eastern half of the European continent went quickly from the halcyon moments of communism's demise into the extraordinarily difficult task of emerging from Leninist authoritarianism into anything resembling open, tolerant, competitive societies.

A critical juncture is upon Central and Eastern Europe. If we presume that democracy and capitalism will triumph, we are wrong. Even together, they are not self-sustaining. Czechoslovakia in 1938 was the surviving democracy of the region and a well-performing free market economy. But Czechoslovakia was insecure. Chamberlain's pitiful waving of a paper on which he had procured Hitler's signature at Munich evinces a powerful truth—without security, democracy and free markets mean little.

In 1993, erstwhile Communist party states in Europe exist in a threat-rich and capacity-poor environment. They lack both individually or collectively the economic, political, or military capacities to balance threats from within and outside. There are very few instances where one could plausibly see any scenario for one state's aggression against another; armies are not massed on borders, and capabilities to mount cross-border conventional invasions are very limited. Yet, there are palpable dangers to nations, states, and governments throughout the region from extremist political movements, volatile labor relations, ethnic hatreds, fragile civilian control over military and police, and popular antipathy toward the pain of being inflicted by market-creating adjustments. People at the top and the bottom do not feel safe, certain, or confident. Demagogues thrive on such nutrients, identifying scapegoats, fanning intolerance, and indicting democrats as a peril to the nation and state.

In the Working Group's report on "Unfinished Revolutions," policy guidance is offered about a transformation that will never succeed unless security is first provided. The dynamic balance between threats and capacities that is the essence of security cannot now be achieved through the indigenous efforts of post-Communist Europe. Instead, such a milieu, within which free market democracies can be nurtured, ought to be the first goal of U.S. and Western policy.

Part of that security is, indeed, economic. "Unfinished Revolutions" notes accurately that new governments and their market reforms are being rejected because of high social costs, which can be mitigated through better targeted assistance.

But a larger and prior security is political and military. Democracies generally have not developed in environments other than those that are devoid of imminent peril due to isolation or insulation, or protected from peril by a larger hegemon. This is no accident, since the tolerance and accommodation, embedded in laws and institutions, must be nurtured, taught, and learned over a lengthy period.

The interwoven and highly interdependent processes of institutionalizing democracy, creating a market economy and finding new bases for security are implicit to the Working Group's report. But we should all regard these three goals of post-Communist systems as, at once, coextensive and conflictual: They have to be pursued simultaneously, but exist side by side with considerable friction. The high political and social costs of economic reform and the security dependence of both democracy and market should always guide our policy.

What, then, does this mean for U.S. and Western policy? First, it ought to mean that we see shock therapy as a route to capitalism as of dubious value when the cost is political turmoil and social upheaval. We should invest in mitigating the pain of such a transformation, not an instantaneous one. We want to see free market democracies in Europe's eastern half at the beginning of the 21st century more than we need to see such systems three years after the unraveling of Communist party control. And, in the intervening years, it is more important to us that the political capital of democracy not be exhausted prematurely because of hemorrhaging legitimacy.

Most important, however, we need to provide security. We need to open a security umbrella, not just display a closed one, as NATO has done with the North Atlantic Cooperation Council (NACC). Let's either quickly extend NATO or, as I have argued elsewhere, recognize that the venerable alliance for common defense needs a robust partner for regional collective security—an invigorated son-of-CSCE. Had we not spent 1989-91 opposing a strengthening of CSCE, the Euro-Atlantic Community might have had the means with which to engage in peacekeeping in Yugoslavia when there was a peace to keep.

These larger themes of relationships among democracy, market, and security mean a great deal for policy, and ultimately for Americans' peace and well-being. If we do not secure the post-Cold War peace we sacrificed to obtain for 45 years, then none of our hopes for democratic, free-market successor states will last long.